# Advanced Praise

"A must read for women in different stages of the divorce process...a brilliant job of integrating education with heartfelt emotions...authentically from the heart and filled with hope. Wherever you are in your journey, you will feel validated and honored."
—**Louise Griffith MA, founder of One Shining Light, author of** *You Are Worth It: 52 Weeks of Honoring, Loving, and Nurturing Your Soul*

"SO powerful...Barb captures the REAL complexity and resilience of living through divorce. Each vignette is a delightful guide full of deep wisdom...a must read for anyone who has been through transitions and desires to heal, become whole, and realize her full potential."
—**Michele Rae, RPh, MA, NBC-HWC, university professor, founder of The Center Within, author of** *Living From the Center Within: Co-Creating Who You Are Becoming*

"This book is full of insights that encourage you to reframe the struggles that typically come from divorce and turn them into opportunities for personal growth, allowing you to come out stronger on the other side. It's the kind of advice and wisdom you'd get from a best friend."
—**Kat D., experience researcher**

"I wish Barb's book would have been available when my own 20 year marriage ended. As you navigate the sometimes challenging, oftentimes lonely journey, let this book be your compassionate companion."
—**Lisa Bobyak, life balance and leadership coach, founder of Living Fully Balanced**

"Encouraging, comforting, thought provoking, and entertaining…and experience based, making it relatable to all."
—**B. H., divorced after 38 years of marriage**

# THE SEASONS OF DIVORCE

*Insights for Women in Transition*

# THE SEASONS OF DIVORCE

*Insights for Women in Transition*

BARB GREENBERG

Kirk House Publishers

The Seasons of Divorce © Copyright 2020 Barb Greenberg

All rights reserved. No part of this book may be used or reproduced in any manner whatsoever without written permission of the author except in the case of brief quotations embodied in critical articles and reviews.

The information in this book is distributed as an "as is" basis, without warranty. Although every precaution has been taken in the preparation of this work, neither the author nor the publisher shall have any liability to any person or entity with respect to any loss or damage caused or alleged to be caused directly or indirectly by the information contained in this book.

Printed in the United States of America

First Edition
ISBN: 978-1-952976-03-2
Library of Congress Control Number: 2020915175
Cover and Interior Book Design: Ann Aubitz

Published by Kirk House Publishers
1250 E 115th Street
Burnsville, MN 55337
kirkhousepublishers.com
612-781-2816

# Dedication

*This book is dedicated to every woman
on the journey to rediscover herself.*

# Acknowledgments

Thank you to Peg Cowart, who, even though she knows how my mind works, continues to believe in me.

Thank you to Miki Banavige, a.k.a. Sparkles the Clown, and volunteer extraordinaire.

Thank you to my friend and editor, Connie Anderson, who never stopped encouraging me to put this book together, and when I did, she made it better than I ever imagined.

Thank you to Barb Freeman and Kelly Bard, who always support me, give me great feedback, and continue to make me laugh.

Thank you to Christina Kraus, who took the time to polish the manuscript with her keen eye, her insights, and her love of grammar.

Thank you to the women I have met who face their divorce journey with such tremendous courage, strength, and faith in the future. The articles in this book have been inspired by you.

May they be reminders that each of us can weather every season of our life with grace.

# Table of Contents

| | |
|---|---|
| Introduction | \|11 |

## Fall  |13
| | |
|---|---|
| One Woman's Decision | \|15 |
| Falling Leaves | \|18 |
| Seek Understanding | \|20 |
| If You Think You Can, You Can...Really? | \|22 |
| It's Not Failure! | \|24 |
| What Will People Think? | \|26 |
| Presto-Change-O | \|28 |
| Eating Alone | \|30 |
| Do You Know This Woman? | \|33 |
| Anger and the Nice Girl | \|36 |
| Macaroni and Cheese and Creative Avoidance | \|39 |
| Depression: The Journey Down | \|42 |
| Lowering the Bar | \|45 |
| Scared? Me Too! | \|48 |
| Spooky! | \|50 |
| Reflections on the Season | \|53 |

## Winter  |55
| | |
|---|---|
| Beware of Men in Forests Wearing Tights | \|57 |
| Are You Listening? | \|59 |
| The Emotional Roller Coaster | \|61 |
| Facing Fear and Finding Treasures | \|63 |
| Self-Compassion | \|65 |
| Moving Mountains | \|67 |
| Stories Carved in Stone | \|69 |
| Beauty and the Beast | \|71 |
| It's Not Fair! | \|73 |
| The Trivia Question | \|75 |
| The Stolen Wallet | \|77 |
| GPS for Your Life | \|80 |
| Warming Up to Fear | \|82 |
| Healthy Boundaries | \|84 |
| Forgiveness | \|86 |
| The Campfire | \|88 |
| Reflections of the Season | \|90 |

## Spring | 93
- Superpowers | 95
- Waking Up Sleeping Beauty | 97
- The "Be Mine" Candy Heart | 99
- Expect a "Visit" | 101
- Be Honest with Yourself | 103
- Who Am I Without All My Stuff?! | 105
- Finding Your Voice | 107
- Dreaming Girl | 109
- Do We Have Self-Esteem Backwards? | 111
- Rent or Own My Life?! | 114
- What Does Healing Really Look Like? | 116
- Self-Love...You're Kidding, Right?! | 118
- You're Confused? Hooray! | 120
- It's Not That Bad | 122
- Being at Ease in Your Own Life | 124
- Release | 126
- Forgiveness and Fishing | 128
- Finding Peace Within | 130
- Reflections of the Season | 133

## Summer | 135
- Butterfly Sightings | 137
- Tubing Down the River | 139
- Taking off the Training Wheels | 142
- Enjoy Looking Up | 144
- Untangling Truth from Fear | 146
- Independence Day | 148
- County Fair | 150
- Healing on a Stick? | 152
- I'm So Proud of Myself | 154
- The Possibilities of Recreating Yourself | 156
- Joy and Finding Frogs! | 158
- The Artist in You | 160
- Rush Hour | 162
- Shine Your Light | 164
- A Most Powerful Resolution | 166
- The Baby Shower Gift | 168
- Open the Windows | 170
- Reflections of the Season | 172
- Honoring You | 175

# Introduction

I was married for thirty-three years.

During my divorce and for some time after this painful process, if anyone would have dared to say there was a wonderful life waiting for me, I would have smacked them. It turns out they would have been right, which doesn't mean I'm relaxing on a beach somewhere with a small paper umbrella in my drink!

There are still times I come face-to-face with painful emotions, get confused and frustrated, and make lots of mistakes, some of which have been doozies.

Yet, the seasons of life forever cycle. Some years they are very mild, and we barely notice them. Other times they rush at us full force and take our breath away. And so it is with divorce.

*In the fall, the life we have
known literally falls away
from us.
Winters are dark and cold,
yet life remains, often unseen,
deep under the frozen earth.
Spring offers hope for new
beginnings, and
in summer we are able
to blossom.*

We Minnesotans know that the weather never fits neatly into four seasons, especially after we've seen it snow in May—and women dealing with divorce know the weather of our lives is often uncertain. There are experiences that chill us to the bone and others that offer sunlight and warmth when we least expect it.

My hope is that this compilation of articles offers support for your divorce journey and reminds you that you are not alone. May the questions at the end of each article offer you prompts for journaling or for conversations with trusted friends. May your answers, or the additional questions you begin to ask yourself, give you a deeper understanding of the seasons of your life and your history, and illuminate the path on which you find yourself.

# Fall

# One Woman's Decision

Once upon a time, a couple planned a much-anticipated road trip. The sky was a perfect blue, the temperature was mild, and the road was so inviting, leading to a mountain lush with tall evergreens and punctured with jagged boulders that didn't seem threatening from a distance.

With the husband behind the wheel of a big, solid car, and the wife in the passenger seat, the loving couple kissed and smiled and were on their way. The paved road turned to gravel as it approached the mountain and was soon a narrow dirt ribbon curling along the rugged mountain's edge, barely wide enough for their car.

When the wife looked ahead through the windshield, she saw that the road was punctured with tips of boulders poking up through the dirt, as if the mountain did not want to give up any part of its sacred space. She saw how narrow the road was and didn't want to imagine what would happen if another car approached coming from the other direction. Frightened, she looked to her left, past the profile of her husband, and saw the unyielding mountainside blocking out the sky. She looked to her right and saw only open space to fall into, imagining the tops of the evergreens far below being the sole witness to her descent if he wasn't careful.

"Slow down," she said to her husband, a habitual speeder.

The husband did not respond and maneuvered another curve around the mountain edge.

"Slow down," she repeated in a panic.

Again the husband did not respond.

She pleaded. She screamed. White-knuckled, she held onto the door handle, as if holding tightly would save her if they plunged over the side.

Eventually, the mountain plateaued, the road widened in front of them, and the terrifying ride was over. The husband explained he was rushing to keep up with a car that was in front of them. The wife never saw another car and didn't believe him.

Years later, she shared this story with a friend who asked, "Why didn't you just get out?"

She was embarrassed to admit she had never thought she could get out—and wondered what dangers she would have faced alone on a mountain road in the middle of nowhere.

Yet, three years later, she did get out—out of a marriage where her feelings and her voice were not acknowledged or respected. She got out of a situation where she thought she would fall off the edge of her life, never to be found.

She stepped tentatively onto a road she never imagined. Eventually, she stood firmly on the mountain that was a part of her journey. The mountain held her, and she felt its strength. Feeling safe at last, she could see the beauty of the vista stretching out before her. She knew there might be danger, and that at times she might stumble, but she was no longer afraid of these things.

Well, sometimes she is…and that's okay. Her future might be unknown, but it is her future.

### Ask yourself:

- No matter who initiated the divorce, how can I, or did I, find the courage to leave and stand in a new place in my life?

- What am I most afraid of when I look to the future?

- What am I most hopeful about when I look to the future?

# Falling Leaves

I remember autumn leaves scattered on the ground. Most had become brown and brittle. Others were still vibrantly red and yellow, as if they had not yet been ready to fall from the branches of their summer home. I imagined they no longer recognized the world around them as chilly winds scattered them across lawns and sidewalks, far from the places they once knew.

When my divorce process began, I, too, noticed that the familiar places of my life had either disappeared completely or had become unrecognizable. My sense of security had blown away. Friends who felt they had to choose sides fell out of my life. Like the last of the leaves floating to earth, I let go in despair, asking, "How did I not see what was happening? How did I not know?" I had been shaken to my core, and all that remained were the dark, bare branches of my life, vulnerable and empty.

I could not imagine that I would survive the approaching winter of my life, even though I knew spring always returns with hope and possibilities.

Over the years, I've shifted my focus from the fallen leaves and have begun to identify with the branches: some graceful, some twisted with age. Branches that seemed bare and dark fill every spring with buds that open and unfold into lush green leaves, rich and textured, shimmering in the sun and swaying in the soft breeze.

These branches would not have been able to hold this new life if the old had remained.

Though sometimes change still shakes me to my core, seeing the branches and the trees that support them, rooted deeply in the earth, I am quietly reminded that life will always renew itself.

### Ask yourself:

- What do I miss the most that has fallen away from my life?

- What parts of my life have been the hardest to let go of, and why?

- What helps me trust that my life will bloom again?

# Seek Understanding

I'd always heard that "knowledge is power," and it's fairly easy to accumulate knowledge. All you have to do is Google a request or reach out to an attorney, financial planner, therapist, or a good friend.

Then I read that "understanding has more power than knowledge." Could that be? Understanding does seem to offer something more, a deeper sense of things.

Understanding is not as easy to find as knowledge, and it never occurred to me that it was something my divorce journey would teach me.

Each of us is on a classic heroine's journey. It begins by being separated from what we know and what we have believed about ourselves, our situation, and our future. Then comes the dark night of the soul, the going down into oneself. Finally, we return with lost and long-forgotten insights and powers to help heal ourselves and others.

You are the heroine of your own story. You are rescuing yourself, rediscovering your light, your wisdom, your treasures, your talents, and your joy.

*Ask yourself:*

- What am I discovering on my journey down into myself?

- What are the most important things my divorce journey is helping me understand?

- What does it mean to be the heroine of my own story?

# IF YOU THINK YOU CAN, YOU CAN...REALLY?

"If you think you can, you can, and if you think you can't, you're right."

I've heard this motivational quote, or something similar to it, more times than I can count—and it really irritates me!

Thinking you can save your marriage doesn't happen if you're the only one working on the relationship. Thinking you can protect yourself or your children from difficult situations is not always possible, and no matter how often you think about it, getting everything you want in a divorce settlement is rare.

So, if you think you can and you can't, what happens?

If you are the only one working on your marriage, it is a sign that the marriage is already over, which can provide clarity. Difficult situations can teach our children, and us, how to become more resilient, create healthy boundaries, and reconnect to our intuition. Not getting everything we want can be an incredible gift because it makes us reflect on what truly holds value for us.

Although it is not unusual to think that you can't survive your divorce, most women not only survive; they thrive and create a new future filled with possibilities.

And though there are many wonderful motivational quotes, be aware of which you choose to inspire you. Sometimes it is not about the voice in your head and how you choose to think. Sometimes it's about the voice from your heart—and what you choose to do.

- What truly holds value for me?

- When I listen, what is my heart telling me?

- What motivational quote inspires me, even in the darkest times, and why?

# It's Not Failure!

Failure is not a word that fits for much of life because too much judgment oozes from it.

Have you ever heard someone say she felt like a failure because she was divorced or was in the process of divorcing? Have you ever felt like that yourself?

Maybe your marriage didn't work and couldn't last. Maybe you tried desperately to keep it together, yet you felt for a long time that something wasn't right, or maybe you were blindsided and shocked when your partner announced he was leaving and it was over.

Whatever caused your divorce process to begin, you can find yourself overwhelmed by pain, fear, grief, and confusion.

Why would anyone judge this very personal situation as if it were a grade on a report card? This is a time and place where people are struggling to find their way. It's not a failure. It's life, and life is filled with choices and changes—and also with loss and with grace.

Often people say that things happen for a reason. Whether you believe this or not, when you are ready, you can create a reason for what happened. When you have sufficiently recovered from your divorce (or any life trauma), you can choose to grow, to learn, and to make a difference in some way.

Ultimately, you can make the choice to be more compassionate with yourself and with others and strive to heal and look to the future.

We are always falling down and getting up. We are always bumping into old thoughts—and what we believed to be certainties—that no longer serve us. This is not failure. It's growth. It's change. It's a gift.

### *Ask yourself:*

- In what ways am I judging myself?

- What old thoughts and beliefs are no longer serving me?

- What new thoughts and beliefs have I decided to embrace, and how do they serve me?

# What Will People Think?

For way too long, I've looked to others to validate my self-worth. Now that I'm divorcing, I can't imagine what "they" must be thinking. I'm certain "they" are judging me—and thus, I feel like I'm drowning in shame. The sofa becomes my lifeboat. I climb onto it and curl up, mumbling and scaring my cat.

I've always given these judgments—whether mine or others, whether real or imagined—tremendous power to undermine my already shaky self-worth. Then, of course, I've judged myself by what I thought others were thinking. It's an exhausting way to go through life. Eventually, I realized that no one was really paying much attention to me anyway!

By reacting to what I assumed everyone else was thinking, I had become disconnected from myself. I sensed that when I did reconnect to who I was, even for moments at a time, my shame would be replaced by compassion, and compassion would be the beginning of my journey back to myself.

Why is being kind to myself such a foreign concept? I'm sure I could list lots of reasons, but instead, I'm going to give myself a hug and go for a walk.

*Ask yourself:*

- Why have I given other people's judgments or expectations power over me?

- How have these judgments caused me to disconnect from myself?

- How can I reconnect to, or how have I reconnected with, myself?

# Presto-Change-O

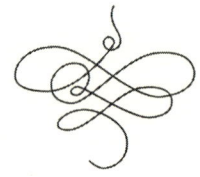

Do you ever have the feeling you are disappearing or have already completely disappeared?

I certainly did, but I didn't disappear all at once like a magic trick: "Presto-change-o. You're gone!"

It happened slowly over time, and it happens to many of us, especially if we're in a relationship where we've been ignored, belittled, or abused in any way.

To me, it felt like I had a form of leprosy—as if small pieces of myself had started to fall away—but I was so busy trying to keep the peace and not rock the boat that I barely noticed.

Then one day, I looked in the mirror, and I was mostly gone. "What happened?" I cried.

I searched for those lost pieces and tried to reattach them as if they were a nose or an ear or a part of an eyebrow. But now they felt awkward, and I sadly wondered if I didn't really deserve them anymore. After all, I'd been getting along without them, and they took up so much room on my face.

But I did deserve them, and I really hadn't been getting along without them at all. As for taking up too much room, how much room should a person take up?

We each deserve to recover those lost pieces of ourselves: our voice, our spirit, our creativity, our joys, our hopes. They are our birthright. They are waiting patiently to return to us, offering us the opportunity to be whole again, and there is no better gift we can give ourselves than this.

## Ask yourself:

- What are the most important pieces of myself that I have lost?

- How has this loss affected my life?

- Where can I find these lost pieces and become whole again—or maybe whole for the first time?

# Eating Alone

One afternoon, searching for the courage to get divorced, I drove alone to a small restaurant about thirty minutes out of the city. It seemed safe. I couldn't imagine bumping into anyone I knew, and when I arrived at about five o'clock, only two other tables were occupied.

The young hostess approached me with menus in the crook of her arm.

"Just one," I said.

"Just one," she repeated, leading me to a small table.

*Just one*, I thought with a sigh, as if one isn't really enough. It doesn't count. It is "less than." Parties of two have substance. Larger parties are impressive, especially when the staff has to move tables together to accommodate all the people. But I'm "just one."

I wondered if being "just one" would be enough. Could I separate those two words, "just" and "one"? Had I ever been able to do that? I couldn't remember.

After the waitress took my order, I ignored the journal I had brought with me to write in and instead bent down and pulled a book out of my oversized purse. Holding it in front of me, I peeked over the top, looking around the restaurant like I was on a military maneuver. The terrain seemed safe, with no hostile activity.

I wasn't very good at eating alone. I imagined people thinking, "Oh, look at the poor lady eating by herself. She must be so lonely."

Yes, I was...more than they could ever imagine.

Eating alone was going to take practice—and so was being alone—if I chose to divorce, though I'd felt more alone in my marriage than I had been willing to admit.

That evening, I understood my decision to divorce had already been made a long time ago, and it was time to acknowledge and honor it, no matter how painful.

Reaching out for help and support would be another thing I'd need to practice, since I had always assumed I had to do everything myself. However, divorce is something no one can do alone.

Although some old friends would shift away from me, others appeared, bringing with them love, a willingness to listen, extra tissues, chocolate, and even laughter—and I knew in my heart I was not alone.

With their help, I learned that I am not "*just* one," and neither are you. You are one bold, strong, brave, courageous woman.

## Ask yourself:

- What changes in my life will I need to practice, and how will I practice them?

- What reassures me that "one" is more than enough and that I am more than enough?

- In what ways am I bold, strong, brave, and courageous and what, if anything, makes me think I am not?

# Do You Know This Woman?

She knew divorcing was not for the faint of heart and deeply doubted her ability to accomplish such a feat, but she could no longer ignore the fact that her marriage was destroying her.

When her husband was critical or harsh, she made excuses for him. The days he was determined to prove her wrong with a prolonged discourse that lacked only the PowerPoint presentation, she still believed he had her best interest at heart.

When she did manage to stand up for herself, she was knocked down with a short, sharp comment, a sigh of exasperation, or criticism veiled in a joke. If she dared to complain, she was told she was being too sensitive.

Because there was no yelling, she never considered this to be verbal abuse. Because the bruises were invisible, she never saw the bloody evidence of his attacks.

Having been taught to find the good in people and always give others the benefit of the doubt, she did not recognize the damage he was inflicting and had no skills to defend herself even if she had.

Eventually, she stopped offering opinions or sharing feelings. They were certain to be analyzed, found lacking, and brushed aside like lint off of a business suit. She didn't recognize the point at which she stopped trusting herself, but rather she began to fade like an old photograph—and she applied her smile like lipstick since it no longer originated from her spirit.

It was time for her to admit that self-worth is non-negotiable, and deserting herself in order to maintain a relationship was no longer acceptable. She retained an attorney, filed for divorce, and moved into a small apartment, expecting to feel excruciatingly alone. Instead, she felt the safest she had in years.

In this space, she tended to a flood of raw emotions. Tremendous sorrow washed over her. Extreme anger crashed around her. She struggled to make it through each day, exhausted and doing her best not to drown.

In the midst of this swirling chaos, healing began with glimmers of courage and hope. She had not completely disappeared but was hanging on by her fingernails. It was time to rescue herself, and no super hero can compete with a woman on a mission to bring herself back from the brink of extinction.

*Ask yourself:*

- What helps me make it through each day?

- How am I learning to trust myself again, or maybe for the first time?

- How do I begin, or continue, to rescue myself?

# Anger and the Nice Girl

I was really good at being sad; I was really *not* good at being angry. Nice girls don't get angry, and I had always done my best to be a nice girl.

My therapist insisted I needed to connect with my anger and suggested I scribble my anger with dark-colored crayons on a large piece of paper. It sounded easy and rather silly, but the first time I did it, I turned my head away as I scribbled, afraid to look at what I was expressing.

I also wrote "those letters" to my ex—the ones you are never supposed to send, the ones where you swear and yell and scream on paper and *tell him, if you haven't already, what you really think!*

One day I began yet another letter and realized I was simply going to repeat what I had already written over and over and over in my ever-growing unsent stash, and it was getting boring.

I changed my mind and wrote to my anger instead.

*Dear Anger,*

*What's the deal anyway?*

As I wrote, it became clear to me that my anger was a valuable emotion. It was a tool I had never been allowed to access. It shouted, "Something is not right," and gave me the energy to get off the sofa and move forward.

I think anger has gotten a bad reputation, partly because many of us never learned the most effective way to use it. When we find the energy to get off the sofa, we must decide what to do with our anger, and unfortunately, we do not always make the wisest choices.

- We turn our anger against ourselves, which is not helpful.
- We whine, which is often described as anger coming through a very small opening, and that doesn't help.
- If there was a betrayal, we may focus our anger at the other person involved, but the other person was not the one who made the commitment to love and cherish us. Our spouse did.
- We "lose it" and rage and scream at others, making so much noise that no one can really hear what we're trying to say.

At the beginning of my divorce, I remember a particular meeting with a therapist and my soon-to-be ex. When it was over, I was so angry that I got into my car, slammed the driver's side door shut, and in the privacy of my Grand Am, where no one could hear me, I did scream and didn't stop for the entire thirty-minute drive home.

I had definitely connected to my anger. This was one of the turning points in the maze that was my divorce. My anger was no longer silent. It was forcing me to pay attention and making it clear I needed to take action.

What action could this be? I had no idea. I didn't think pushing my ex off a bridge was an option, so I focused on making the best decisions I could to honor myself and my future, and in that process, I hoped to find peace and to understand myself more fully.

## *Ask yourself:*

- In what ways am I using my anger against my ex, or against myself, that are not effective?

- What has been, or can be, the most effective use of my anger?

- What has my anger taught me?

# Macaroni and Cheese and Creative Avoidance

Some days, there was nothing more important to me than finding relief from the stress and pressure of my divorce.

I wasn't a drinker. I didn't like to shop. I didn't have the energy to keep busy with errands and checking things off my to-do list, which is at least a productive form of avoidance.

Still, I managed to find a solution. I ate bowls and bowls of my favorite comfort food, macaroni and cheese. It filled me up and made me drowsy. Shoveling forkfuls into my mouth distracted me and was my salvation until it became clear that no amount of those orange starchy noodles was going to ease my grief.

So, I created a new strategy. I began watching really bad TV, and to feel productive while I sat in front of the screen, I decided to knit a sweater. I kept knitting and knitting, and the sweater got longer and longer, until I realized there was not enough yarn to fill the void in my life.

Putting down the knitting needles, I was once again overcome by an avalanche of emotions and realized that trying to outrun them was hopeless. Even though I was terrified they would bury me, I understood the only way to save my life was to turn and face what I was running from.

It took a lot of therapy and a lot of tissues, but I began to realize that distractions are not the same as comfort—and I needed comfort. Where could I possibly find it? I was too drained to comfort myself and too exhausted to search for it, but turns out I didn't have to search. I began to notice that when the cat curled up on my lap, when I opened the windows and heard a bird sing, when I stepped outside and felt the warmth of the sun, it was there.

Slowly my pain began to ease. I could face my emotions without squeezing my eyes shut as if I was watching a scary movie. I realized that being sad, angry, depressed, or frightened didn't make me weak, lazy, selfish, or any other label I wanted to put around my neck. My emotions made me human. They made me honest.

I had spent too many years pretending things were fine when they were not as they should have been.

## Ask yourself:

- What things have I been running from, and how can I face them?

- What was, or is, the most important thing I needed, or need, to be honest about, and why?

- What happened, or what do I feel will happen, when I am honest?

# Depression: The Journey Down

I had been curling up on the sofa for daily naps. It didn't feel ominous; it felt safe, like I was climbing onto a lifeboat every afternoon.

Why did I need a lifeboat? What was sinking? I was. I felt nauseous when I ate. I felt dizzy when I didn't eat. I felt like crying all the time, but I couldn't cry enough. I had constant headaches that sparkled behind my eyes. I couldn't make decisions because if I made the wrong decision, something terrible would happen. It was clear to me that something was very wrong.

I made an appointment with a soft-spoken psychologist, who confirmed that I had classic signs of situational depression.

**If you are struggling with symptoms of depression, please reach out for help.**

At the end of our session, she did not recommend medication. Instead, she told me that my body was wiser than I was and that if it was insisting that I sit on the sofa, that is exactly what I should do.

At first, I was grateful that there was a name for what was happening to me—situational depression, but my relief was swiftly followed by a now-familiar fear. I felt as if I was dropping down a miles-deep canyon, no bottom, only nothingness, and nothing to grab hold of to stop my fall.

I panicked. "I can't be depressed. It means I'm weak. I'm a failure. Why can't I control this? Just get up and move. Please just get up." I couldn't.

I was afraid of turning into the lady with the pink fuzzy slippers and the ratty bathrobe who sat with the TV remote control in one hand and a Twinkie in the other. If I wasn't doing something, I was certain I had no value. I was defective. I couldn't believe there was integrity in just "being." I was convinced that if I heard voices, they would tell me what to do to change the world. They wouldn't tell me to sit on the sofa. They would call me to action, not insist that I rest.

In our culture, it is acceptable to go "up the ladder of success" and to go "out into the world." But to stop and go down into ourselves can be terrifying, yet it is a sacred journey. It is where we find the pieces of ourselves that have been lost or broken, and we can gently bring them back up into the light and begin the process of becoming whole once more.

## *Ask yourself:*

- What do I learn when I listen to my body?

- Have I felt that I needed to be doing something to be of value, and if so, why?

- What value have I found in simply "being"?

# Lowering the Bar

A friend treated me to dinner at a neighborhood pizza place to offer support as I was struggling through my divorce. In between bites of a delicious, cheesy slice of pizza, I moaned about my painful situation.

"I can't do this. It's too hard. I'm not handling this well at all. Really, I'm not handling this well at *all!*"

With a knowing smile, my friend asked, "Are you getting out of bed in the morning?"

"Yes."

"Then you're handling it!"

Well, I had been hoping I could set the bar a little higher for myself. I took her words to heart and discovered, surprisingly, that I could make more progress without the pressure of that bar.

My ego was not happy and hollered, "You can't do that! What's wrong with you? You are being irresponsible. You need that bar!"

While my ego ranted, I could feel that my spirit was grateful, and so was my body.

Lowering the bar eased the pressure I was putting on myself and lowered my stress level, which I have no doubt kept me healthy.

Lowering the bar gave me permission to slow down. I'd heard TV commercials for internet connections proclaiming that "fast" is so much better than "slow." That may be true for internet connections, but not for healing from divorce.

Lowering the bar allowed me to reimagine my journey. In the past, I'd had an image of traveling "the road of life." Now the road seemed hard and dusty, filled with dangerous twists and turns, and if I stayed on this road, I had to keep moving or be run over by whatever was coming up behind me.

One day I read that life isn't a road—it's a meadow. I loved that image. It felt soft and fragrant, and I could sit and rest when needed. Maybe the road I had been on led me to this meadow.

I am now considering eliminating the bar altogether. I could put it in a corner and decorate it with bright streamers, I could build a ladder to use when I'm ready to climb back into life, or I may break it into pieces, use it as firewood, and build a fire to warm myself and lighten the darkness.

## Ask yourself:

- What bars in my life need to be lowered, and what can I do to lower them?

- What are the voices of resistance I hear when I begin to lower bars, and how can I respond to them?

- How will lowering bars affect me mentally, emotionally, and spiritually?

# Scared? Me Too!

I was afraid of being alone, of not having the ability to support myself—and of the pain I was causing my children. I was afraid I was not eating enough or was eating too much. I was afraid my jeans made me look fat. I was afraid of the unknown. I was even afraid my mother would come over before I had time to clean my bathroom.

And the fear that I would never stop crying or be able to move forward with my life covered me like a heavy, grimy, gray blanket.

Affirmations didn't help, and I couldn't find a positive attitude no matter how hard I looked. In fact, I felt bullied by a culture that promoted "positive thinking." Positive thinking can be very helpful, but I was not ready to be helped.

I wanted all my emotions to be acknowledged, to be respected, and not to be glossed over and photoshopped so they would be acceptable. If I allowed that to happen, I would be betraying myself. I would feel like a fraud and worse. By not speaking my truth, I would be perpetuating an atmosphere that denied other women permission to speak their truth.

After tossing and turning one sleepless night, I turned on the bedroom light, found a legal pad and a pen, and began to scribble. "I'm scared. I'm scared. I'm *&#! scared."

Sometimes I pressed so hard with my pen it ripped through the paper. Sometimes I wrote so wildly that one sentence took up an entire page. When I had used up every sheet in the pad, I put it down, placed the pen on top of it, turned off the light, crawled back into bed…and slept like a baby.

What a relief it was to stop trying to hold it all together. How refreshing it was to be totally honest with myself. I moved from feeling betrayed and discarded to knowing I would survive—and that I had more power than I realized.

## Ask yourself:

- What things do I fear the most?

- How can I, or do I, release my fears?

- What are the healthiest ways I've found to acknowledge all of my emotions?

# Spooky!

Halloween was just a few days away, bringing back childhood memories of trick or treating in homemade costumes on chilly evenings, bags filled with candies from generous neighbors, and running home to sit on the living room floor to sort out my favorites.

I had been invited to go out with friends on the Saturday before Halloween and was told I had to wear a costume, something I hadn't done in twenty years. I rebelled and was simply going to wear a nice pair of jeans and a cute sweater...boring, I know. When my friends found this out, they insisted that my plan was not an option and that I needed to stop by their home early that evening, gleefully announcing they would have something special for me to wear. Their enthusiasm made me quite nervous. I couldn't imagine what they had in mind.

Then I realized something spooky. Many of us were married to a spouse who was always in disguise and who hid his true self behind a mask.

Even more frightening was that many of us began to wear our own disguises, especially if we were in emotionally, or physically, dangerous relationships. We disguised our feelings and our thoughts to keep peace and to protect ourselves. We believed this would keep us safe, but we were wrong. And we began to disappear.

It takes tremendous courage to take off our masks and see who we really are.

The trick is to trust how we truly feel and what we instinctively know. The treat is that we will rediscover our authentic self.

Then we can dress ourselves, not in disguises that hide us, but in costumes that reflect our true spirit. We can delight as the glitter in our hair catches the light and enjoy how cool we feel when we spin and our cape twirls around us.

We all have the power of Wonder Woman, the grace of a princess, and the ability to transform like a butterfly.

My costume that Saturday night was Spider-Woman. In many Native American traditions, the spider is a reminder that we are the weavers of our own destiny, and we have the ability to weave together the past and the future to create delicate yet extraordinarily strong threads that sparkle when touched by the sun.

## *Ask yourself:*

- If I wore disguises, what were they, and why did I feel I needed to wear them?

- If my spouse wore disguises, what were they, how did I discover them, and what happened when I did?

- What are the "costumes" that express my true spirit, and why have I chosen them?

# Reflections of the Season

*Her future might be unknown, but it is her future.*

*I am quietly reminded that life will always renew itself.*

*Sometimes it's not about the voice in your head and what you chose to think. Sometimes it's about the voice in your heart and what you choose to do.*

*Why is being kind to myself such a foreign concept? I'm sure I could list lots of reasons, but instead, I'm going to give myself a hug and go for a walk.*

*We each deserve to recover those lost pieces of ourselves: our voice, our spirit, our creativity, our joys, our hopes.*

*I learned that I am not "just one," and neither are you. You are one bold, strong, brave, courageous woman.*

*No superhero can compete with a woman on a mission to bring herself back from the brink of extinction.*

*I understood the only way to save myself was to turn and face what I was running from.*

*My emotions made me human. They made me honest. Now honesty was the greatest gift I could give myself.*

*We all have the power of Wonder Woman, the grace of a princess, and the ability to transform like a butterfly.*

# Winter

# Beware of Men in Forests Wearing Tights

The handsome fairytale princes I remember reading about had great hair, rode powerful white horses, and wore tights.

I have no idea why they were spending so much time in a forest. They might have been lost or taking a shortcut back to the palace from a royal conference.

Once upon a time, while on his ride, a prince came across Snow White asleep on a bed of flowers. Once upon another time, a different prince, while riding along, found the palace where Sleeping Beauty was, you guessed it, asleep.

Sadly, neither Snow White nor Sleeping Beauty realized she had the power to wake herself, and neither one was aware of what might not be so charming when it came to a relationship with a prince.

So, my dear, here are a few warning signs of danger; for forests and palaces are not the only places where you can fall asleep.

When you are awakened by a handsome prince...

- Beware of an overabundance of charm.
- Beware of a relationship that moves too quickly and doesn't give you any time to think.
- Beware of any prince who wants to isolate you, even if it's in his glorious palace.
- Beware of any prince who prevents you from making your own decisions and discourages you from seeing friends and family.
- Beware of a prince who does not respect your opinions and assumes that he is always right because, after all, he is the prince.
- Beware that you are not running to the prince because you think he will rescue you from a wicked stepmother or other past pain you have not resolved.

Whether you have lived in the comfort of an elegant palace with rooms draped in heavy tapestries or you have felt at home in the wilds of a forest thick with towering oak trees, a princess must always remember to stay awake and to honor and respect her unique and powerful self.

## Ask yourself:

- If my prince wasn't so charming, how and why did I miss the warning signs?

- How is my divorce helping me to wake up?

- What have I decided to do to honor and respect myself?

# Are You Listening?

"Look what he did to me!"

This became my mantra during and after my divorce. My heart, my spirit, and my finances were all in jeopardy of being damaged beyond repair. I was miserable and repeated my mantra often. Each time I did, my friends gave me a hug and another dose of sympathy.

Then in the middle of the night, a very loud and clear voice woke me from a deep sleep.

"Not acceptable, Bucko," was all it said. It didn't sound like the voice of an angel. I didn't think angels even used the word "Bucko," but it worked.

It was time to take responsibility for my future, which seemed to be an overwhelming, daunting, and terrifying task. Even so, I stopped looking at what he did to me and began deciding what I would do for myself.

My previous job was no longer an option for me. I tried substitute teaching, and to no one's surprise, it wasn't a fit. Next, I interviewed for a job in retail, and when I didn't get it, all I could do was mutter, "What's going on?"

Each attempt exhausted me. Nothing seemed to be working. Yet every once in a while, in the midst of all my frustration, I saw a glimmer of hope, something that I wouldn't have been able to see before. I saw something else that stunned me. By staying miserable in order to gain sympathy, I had given control of my life back to my ex, and that was certainly not a fair exchange at all.

Many of us have good reasons to be angry, resentful, and miserable, and it's important to honor these feelings. It's also important to honor the voice that lets us know when it's time to move forward. It may call you Bucko or Sweetie Pie, Dear Heart, or Hey You! Whether it's loud and clear or a gentle whisper, please honor this call to move forward and experience the gifts that are waiting for you.

## *Ask yourself:*

- In what ways am I, or was I, giving my power away to my ex?

- What helped me to see that it was time to "move forward"?

- In what ways do I feel I'm being guided?

# The Emotional Roller Coaster

Whether you love riding roller coasters or want to stay as far away from them as possible, the emotional roller coaster of divorce can take your breath away. You fly from grief, to ultimate rage, to confidence, to depression, to determination with such force that it makes your stomach flip. When I was divorcing, some days I could swing through this cycle three or four times before breakfast.

Please know that you are not alone, you have not lost your mind, and sometimes, like a roller coaster ride, all you can do is hang on.

And when you do, interesting things start to happen.

When you are forced to feel all these emotions, you can become honest with yourself, and honesty may be the most important asset you have.

Being honest about your emotions allows you to learn from them. They are powerful teachers, demanding that you pay attention, and forcing you to look back at your history and down into your heart. And your heart will whisper, "You are a survivor. You are strong. You have value. You will no longer be diminished."

*Ask yourself:*

- What are the most valuable lessons my emotions are teaching me?

- What has helped me "hang on" during my emotional roller coaster rides?

- What strengths do I have that keep me from feeling "diminished"?

# Facing Fear and Finding Treasures

*The cave you fear to enter holds the treasures that you seek.*
—Joseph Campbell

A friend shared this quotation with me when I was frustrated, unsure, and feeling lost. My first thought was, *Wow! That's a great message!*

My next thought was, *I don't want to go into a dark, creepy cave where unseen critters scurry across the damp ground. I really don't. Really!*

Maybe I could delegate this job to some unsuspecting person. "You can go into that cave, and when you find the treasures, just bring them out to me." But I've been in dark caves before and understood that this is a place I must enter myself. Friends can encourage and support me, yet it's up to me to step into the unknown and face my fears.

Divorce was one of my darkest caves. It felt like an underground labyrinth. Everywhere I turned, and every path I took led me to another fear: fear of the future, fear of making the wrong decisions, fear of my intense and overwhelming emotions, fear that I would not survive this pain.

Yet, even in the darkness, glimmers of light were always present.

As I wandered through this cave, I began to trip over interestingly shaped rocks. Bending down to look more closely, I realized I had discovered courage, compassion, strength, and hope that had been scattered on the damp ground like jewels from a pirate's treasure chest.

As I picked them up, the dirt and grime that had covered them fell away, and their brilliance became shafts of light in the darkness.

### Ask yourself:

- How does it feel to step into the unknown, and what is this step teaching me?

- Where do the glimmers of light in my cave come from?

- What treasures have I found, and what surprises have I uncovered, exploring my cave?

# Self-Compassion

It is difficult for me to write about self-compassion. I've always been hard on myself, like a tyrannical boss telling an employee that she's never quite measuring up.

I knew there was no shame in feeling gray and dreary instead of constantly acting bright and sunny, though I believed that was expected of me, and if I said enough affirmations, I could change my state of mind. It didn't work.

Then one day, after another overwhelming wave of grief, I began talking to myself, which is not unusual. This time, though, I actually talked back.

"I know you're trying hard to be brave, and I also know you are grieving."

"Yes, I am."

"I'm sorry."

"Thank you."

"Grief can be so painful, can't it?"

"Yes, it can."
"Would you like a hug?"
"Yes, oh, yes."

I felt my grief release and I cried, as I instantly had an image of myself as a little girl jumping into my adult arms and clinging to me.

Now, whenever I feel any difficult emotions, I talk to myself with compassion, and another piece of me knows it's safe to return home.

## Ask yourself:

- What do I usually say when I talk to myself?

- What does self-compassion mean to me?

- What can I say to my painful emotion, and how can I begin to understand where that pain comes from?

# Moving Mountains

*When sleeping women wake,
mountains move.*
—Chinese proverb

I've always loved this quotation, though it never occurred to me to ask why these women had been asleep in the first place, even though I instinctively knew.

Like many others, I'd been silenced in my marriage—and understood that these women only seemed to be sleeping, because I had done the same.

It was their way to protect themselves, for they did not know it was even possible to push away the hand that had silenced them.

In this silence, women begin to fade away. Soon their gifts and their dreams disappear, and all that remains is an outer shell...something that looks like a woman but is not. Eventually, the weight of this hand, and the ramifications of staying silent, become too much to bear.

Yet, we believe that if we speak our truth, it will destroy us. So it often hides, shaking with fear in the shadows and dark corners of our lives.

Then one woman finds the courage to speak her truth, and her truth gives other women the courage to speak theirs—and the mountains begin to move.

The truth can be incredibly hard to say and can be even harder to hear, and although others may ignore it or shame us, the truth remains...and the mountains still move.

*Ask yourself:*

- What truths have I been afraid to speak?

- What truths have been hard for me to hear?

- What happens when mountains move?

# Stories Carved in Stone

On a recent trip, I spent a morning with my family in a national park that protects one of the largest petroglyph (rock carvings) sites in North America.

Walking through rugged terrain under a clear blue New Mexico sky, we could see designs and symbols that had been carved onto volcanic rocks 400–700 years ago by Native Americans and Spanish settlers. Voices from the past were etched into giant black boulders, remaining unchanged for centuries. It was a powerful experience.

Later I wondered which of my stories I had etched in stone—stories about my self-worth, my history, and my place in this world. Do these stories still serve me? Are they true? Are they even mine, or are they the stories of others that I have taken as my own?

In my personal library of stories, I have the classic trilogy: *I Have No Value*; *My Voice Does Not Matter*; and *I Cannot Possibly Follow My Dreams*.

The section of "poor me" stories holds some of my favorites. I take them out whenever I need a good cry or want to feel self-righteous.

Then there is the popular series of "Lack." *There Is Not Enough Love to Go Around* is the first in this series and can cause tremendous grief to those of us dealing with divorce.

Some unhealthy stories are so deeply etched into each of us that, even if we wanted to, we could not remove them. Instead, we can gently acknowledge they are with us and put them back on the shelf.

The most important story is the one that informs all the others. It is about living our lives from a place of love, compassion, and faith. Out of all the stories, this is the one we must etch onto the rugged terrain of our lives.

### Ask yourself:

- What stories no longer serve me, have done the most damage, and may not even be mine?
- What are the most important stories for me?
- What new stories will I tell myself?

# Beauty and the Beast

The other night I curled up in a big chair under a cozy blanket and flipped through TV channels, catching glimpses of car chases and explosions and deranged killers running from police. Ahhh...what passes for entertainment!

Then gratefully, I found a channel showing Disney's charming *Beauty and the Beast*.

I smiled and wondered, *Who doesn't hope that their story will end with a magical kiss that turns a beast into a handsome prince?* Suddenly my mind screeched to a stop, and a voice hollered, "Wait a minute!"

How many of us have believed in that fairytale and learned the hard way that it doesn't work?

How many of us have found ourselves in a relationship where the "Beast" has skillfully hidden behind an engaging smile, polite manners, and loving words, only to reveal himself when we've felt the most vulnerable and trapped?

How many of us, like Belle, have ignored the warnings of our intuition? When Belle first meets the Beast, he frightens her. He is rude, secretive, and brooding. Her intuition tells her he's not such a good guy, but she stays with him anyway. It's hard to blame her because, like so many of us, she was taught to be nice and look for the best in people—but she never learned how to do that without getting into an unhealthy relationship. Belle also thinks she has no option but to stay with him and does not understand there is always another option.

It's true that life had been hard for the Beast. After all, he was cursed, but he chose not to explore what had happened to him and why...and then to learn from this and to heal. We have all had issues in our lives that felt like curses, yet we have taken time to grieve and made efforts to move forward in our lives the best we can, and hopefully, we've discovered many gifts as a result of those efforts.

I sense that when Belle kissed the Beast, he transformed in her eyes only, becoming the man she had hoped he would be, the man she wanted him to be. She may choose to support the Beast with her love, but there will be no "happily ever after" unless the Beast accepts that the inner work of transformation is his alone, just as it is for Belle and for each of us.

## Ask yourself:

- How have fairy tales affected my expectations about relationships?
- How am I learning to trust my intuition?
- What have I learned from the "beasts" in my life?

# It's Not Fair!

Marie's ex-husband and his new sweetie are in Florida, walking on a sandy beach in the warm sun, while she's in Montana walking through blowing snow in an icy parking lot.

Sandy's ex and his sweetie have a new Lexus, while she has a nine-year-old Honda with duct tape holding together a crack in the front bumper.

Janie's ex and his new wife wear the newest Fitbits on their wrists that not only tell time but track all sorts of things, including how many steps they take each day. Janie has a pink sticky note on her bathroom mirror with the words "walk more" written on it.

During divorce, and often for a few years afterward, we all may want to yell, "It's not fair! It's just not fair!" I have to say I got very good at it, and it felt great...for a while.

Eventually, though, it gets boring. We begin to sound like a fan at a ball game screaming when the referee didn't call a foul or should have called a penalty on the other team. This doesn't always happen in sports. It doesn't alway happen in divorce. And life is not a game, though some people act like it is.

People say time heals, but it's not time alone that heals. No matter how much time goes by, there are people who just can't seem to do it.

Time does give us a chance to shift our perspectives and to gratefully realize that we no longer have to walk on eggshells or give away parts of ourselves in order to be loved.

Though once in a while the "not-fair" gremlin may briefly appear for a short visit, we begin to understand that even though we have found ourselves in a place we never imagined, it is a good place, a healing place, a place of possibilities…and that is more than fair.

## Ask yourself:

- As I deal with my divorce, what feels the most not fair, and what feels more than fair?

- How has my perspective shifted?

- What do I feel grateful for, and what new possibilities am I able to see?

# The Trivia Question

While waiting for a friend at a coffee shop, I looked at their trivia question for the day. "In what country did the French horn originate?"

My first thought was, *If I answer this right, I'll get ten cents off my drink!*

My next thought was, *How many trivial things do I focus on while losing touch with what is truly important?* The answer was a lot…especially during my divorce.

*I didn't file those papers in the right place. I said something really stupid to my attorney or my ex, or worst of all, to my children. I didn't fold the laundry. My mortgage company can't find my property insurance information. I went to the grocery store and forgot to buy an onion, and how can I possibly make my casserole without an onion, and oh no, I can't find my car keys.* (They were in the grocery bag!)

I allowed myself to be so smothered in trivia that I no longer noticed what was truly important. And though trivia can be enticing, it was time to change my focus to the adventure of finding what was truly of value in my life.

Where do we look for value and for meaning? It's not on our cell phones, it's not on Google, and it's not on our TV, no matter how big the screen is.

Maybe it's the whisper in our ear, the tap on our shoulder, the shiny sparkle that catches our eye....those things we forget to notice or dismiss as unimportant. I have a sense this is where true meaning waits patiently for us. These things remind us to pause. They remind us to focus on what we hold dear, to evaluate what is precious to us and adds purpose to our lives, and to feel deep gratitude for the gifts of good health, dear friends, and moments of unconditional love.

As for the question, "In what country did the French horn originate?" I have no idea.

*Ask yourself:*

- What trivial things feel like they are smothering me?

- What things are of greatest value in my life?

- What are the things in my life that remind me to pause?

# THE STOLEN WALLET

I was in downtown Minneapolis for a meeting at a coffee shop in a large office building. After the meeting, I went to get my car out of the underground parking lot, and my wallet was not in my purse. I had a sinking feeling in the pit of my stomach, but I kept desperately digging for the familiar feel of it. Maybe it was there. Maybe I was wrong. Maybe all would be back to normal if I could just wrap my hand around that wallet, but it was gone.

I ran back up the escalator to the coffee shop, knowing the wallet wouldn't be there but checking anyway. I ran back down the escalator to the security desk in the building's atrium where a kind, tired security guard helped me find phone numbers for my bank and my credit cards. He then went off duty and walked away. I sat making calls with my cell phone and trying not to scream at the automated voices until I was transferred to a real person in the right department, one of whom said, "Oh yes, someone already tried to charge over $1,000 on your card. Don't worry, it was declined."

I called the police and made a report over the phone. The parking lot attendant let me take my car with no charge, and I drove home on side roads, since I wasn't concentrating well enough to trust myself on the highway.

That night before I fell asleep, I flashed back to the end of my marriage a dozen years ago, and the similarities surprised me.

I had a sinking feeling then too. I desperately hoped things were not as I knew them to be and believed if I could just get a handle on the situation, I could change what had happened. I became exhausted, making phone calls, collecting papers for my attorneys, running to appointments, and fooling myself that I was calmly holding it all together.

It's been three days since my wallet was stolen, and I'm still exhausted. I keep trying to move forward, determined nothing is going to slow me down. But things do slow us down, and we should let them. No matter what the world around us says about the advantages of fast cars, fast food, and fast internet connections, slowing down is vital for healing. It's a form of self-care. I thought I was pretty good at self-care, but during my divorce, nothing I did seemed to help.

I would go for short walks, which would give me a burst of energy, just before I got home and collapsed into my living room chair.

I planned on eating well but was too exhausted to get up and go into the kitchen.

If a motivational book had been nearby and I had the energy, I would have thrown it across the room.

It turns out for me, and maybe for you as well, the best self-care practice is patience.

Having your wallet stolen is nothing compared to having your dreams stolen and having the foundation of your life crumble beneath your feet. So instead of charging forward, I'm doing my best to take the time to sit quietly and be patient.

Fast is fascinating. It allows us to zoom into the world and fly through life. Patience is not nearly as exciting, yet it can take us to places we would not notice if we were going at full speed...places of hope, of healing, of peace.

*Ask yourself:*

- What experiences trigger the difficult memories of my divorce?

- How did it feel, and what did I discover, when I realized I couldn't change what was happening in my marriage?

- When I slow down, what do I notice about myself and about my situation?

# GPS for Your Life

The maze of detours and construction in downtown Minneapolis did not faze my GPS as it took me safely and easily to my destination. I wondered what it would be like if I had a GPS for my life, though often I don't even know where I want to go, let alone how to get there.

It would be very nice to have a calm voice telling me if I should continue following the road I'm on, or let me know that this path will not get me where I need to go and that it's time to change direction. No more confusion, no more frustration, and no more getting lost.

Then I realized I do have a GPS. Even better, I have more than one!

My intuition is always guiding me with its whispers, though sometimes it needs to shout to get my attention. And even then, I don't always listen. I know my body is guiding me whenever I feel that knot in my stomach, that pain in my neck, or those chills down my back. But again, I don't always listen.

As a result, just like my car's GPS, I often have to "recalibrate."

As much as I don't like the effort, and often the pain, that comes with "recalibrating," it is during those times that I learn the most valuable lessons, come to understand compassion at a deeper level, and discover the most extraordinary scenery.

*Ask yourself:*

- How can I, or will I, be able to find direction in my life?

- What feelings come up when I have to "recalibrate"?

- When I have "recalibrated," how did I do it, and what did I learn?

# Warming Up to Fear

It's been a long winter, and I never got around to covering my windows with those clear plastic sheets that are meant to insulate my home and keep out the bitter cold. Instead, I just put on my heaviest sweaters and wonder what else I would like to keep out of my life.

The answer is always the same: fear. Fear can certainly chill me to the bone, and just like cold winter drafts, it can easily keep me in bed, burrowed under my covers. Though I've been repeating affirmations about being fearless, brave, and trusting for years, my fear still makes me shiver, and I need something more effective if I want to warm up.

I read somewhere that we should embrace our fears with compassion—and I decided to give it a try.

The next time I was afraid, instead of responding with an affirmation, I simply listened to my fear. I let it scream and yell and rage on. I did not turn away or try to silence it.

I told it I understood and invited it to sit with me. I told my fear it was loved, and it slowly began to quiet down and eventually curled up and rested against me, almost like a small child who had felt lost and was coming home to be comforted. It simply needed to be heard and acknowledged, and I finally listened without judgment.

I realize now that my fear is a companion, showing up now and then when it needs to. When it appears, we talk with each other, even giggle a bit, and reassure one another that all will be well.

Fear is no longer something to keep out of my life like a cold winter draft. It is a part of me that I have chosen to respect and embrace. When I do, we are both calmed and can find peace.

As for my windows, they are still a little drafty, but when I look through them and out onto the world, I'm now able to see life a little more clearly.

## *Ask yourself:*

- How do I protect myself from the "bitter cold" of my divorce?

- How does it feel, and what do I learn, when I sit with my fear without judgment?

- What other emotions do I want to sit with, and why?

# Healthy Boundaries

When moving through divorce and forward into a new life, we hear a lot about the importance of maintaining healthy boundaries. The idea of boundaries always sounded so empowering to me, though I had no idea what they meant, probably because I never had any!

One day a wise woman offered a simple explanation: "Never walk into the north wind with your coat held wide open." As a native Minnesotan, I understood immediately.

If we do not protect ourselves from the harsh wind, not only can we get physically ill, but we can also become resentful and angry. "Why doesn't this just stop?" We can become anxious and fearful. "Will this ever end?" And when frostbite sets in, we become numb and stop feeling anything.

Many of us don't realize that our coat is open, or we don't realize we have the power to wrap it around ourselves.

Boundaries were very difficult for me to learn. I was taught to value everyone else's interests above my own, and if I didn't, I was being terribly selfish. It was during my divorce that I began to learn that when I did what was best for me, it turned out to be the best for everyone around me.

I came to understand that boundaries are not just for physical safety, but also for our emotional, intellectual, and spiritual integrity. When someone tells us how we should or shouldn't feel, what we should or shouldn't think, or how we should or shouldn't connect with our Higher Power, it is a boundary issue.

Building, maintaining, and adjusting our boundaries is a life-long process that will protect us from whatever the north wind may blow our way.

### Ask yourself:

- What does a healthy boundary look like, especially when dealing with my ex?

- In what areas of my life do I want to create clearer boundaries?

- What are the differences healthy boundaries make, or I hope they will make, in my life?

# Forgiveness

You might have moaned when you saw the word "forgiveness," and I don't blame you.

There seems to be a social expectation that you have to forgive quickly. It assumes that forgiving quickly is a sign of maturity, inner strength, and a reflection of your character. That really bothers me!

This is not a race. How about allowing yourself to be human, to rage and struggle, to be confused and scared, and to wander for a while as you sort through your history? Now that takes true character!

If you and your ex have remained friends, or have become friends, that is wonderful. If your ex has caused you too much pain, or is toxic or dangerous in any way, a friendship is probably not going to happen.

The good news is, that's just fine. Because as you heal, you will eventually come to a place where you still remember your experiences, but the energy around them will have faded. You will be able to be cordial when interacting with your ex and may come to think of this person in the same way you think of, for example, brussels sprouts. No emotion. No drama. Simply, "Yep, I just don't like 'em."

If you can't seem to get to that point, be compassionate with yourself. A dear friend asked her wise eighty-year-old priest if she would ever find forgiveness. He patted her arm and, with a soft smile, said, "You might not. Don't worry about it."

I love this, and it's not as shocking as it sounds. By releasing her of the pressure to forgive, he gave her permission to come to it in her own time.

I believe there is a difference between wanting to forgive and being ready to forgive. I also believe that forgiveness will come to us when we are committed to healing.

## Ask yourself:

- What does forgiveness mean to me?
- What is the difference for me between wanting to forgive and being ready to forgive?
- What do I need to heal to be able to forgive?

# The Campfire

It's evening, and I'm sitting by a campfire. I can see the outline of distant mountains and hear the nearby stream softly tumbling along. The full moon hangs gently in a sky filled with stars. I look at the oversized backpack I have dropped to the ground beside me. For many years I've shouldered this heavy load, and when it was too heavy to carry, or I was too weak, I've dragged it along behind me over rocky terrain.

I can't do it anymore.

I unzip the backpack and watch as the jumbled contents spill out. I don't know if I will survive what I find, as pieces of my history fall to the ground and into the campfire's light: broken dreams, tangles of uncertainty and fear, and sharp edges of grief. I have read that the past is something we take with us. I have also read that the past is something we leave behind.

In truth, this is a decision we each need to make. In this

quiet space, I choose to leave behind the heaviness that no longer serves me. I choose to gather up my stories and notice the gifts embedded in them like veins of gold. These are mine to carry forward, and my load is now lighter, for they no longer hold any blame. Instead, they point the way, leading me to my center, my core.

*Ask yourself:*

- What is the heaviness that I am ready to set down?
- What made me realize that I no longer needed to carry such unbearable weight?
- What are the "veins of gold" that I find in my stories?

# Reflections of the Season...

*I stopped looking at what he did to me and began deciding what I would do for myself.*

*Sometimes, like a roller coaster ride, all you can do is hang on.*

*You are a survivor. You are strong. You have value. You will no longer be diminished.*

*Yet even in the darkness, glimmers of light were always present.*

*Now, whenever I feel grief, sadness, depression, any difficult emotion, I talk to myself with compassion, and another piece of me knows it's safe to return home.*

*The truth can be incredibly hard to say and can even be harder to hear, and although others may ignore or shame us, the truth remains—and the mountains still move.*

*The most important story is the one that informs all the others. It is about living our lives from a place of love, compassion, and faith.*

*It turns out for me, and maybe for you, as well, that the best self-care practice is patience.*

*I began to learn that when I did what was best for me, it turned out to be the best for everyone around me.*

*I choose to gather up my stories and notice the gifts embedded in them like veins of gold. These are mine to carry forward, and my load is now lighter, for they no longer hold any blame.*

# Spring

# Superpowers

My grandson and I went to see the movie *The Incredibles 2*, and ever since, I've been thinking a lot about superpowers.

Stopping a runaway train or steering an out-of-control cruise ship to keep it from crashing into a port city is child's play compared to what so many of us have to handle every day.

Our imaginations run away with us. Our to-do list seems out of control. Pain, grief, and confusion may overwhelm us to the point that getting out of bed in the morning can be considered an act of heroism.

It takes superpowers to search for meaning when we don't think life is fair and to allow our painful circumstances to open, rather than harden, our hearts.

It takes superpowers to be kind to ourselves when we make a mistake, to be kinder to ourselves when we make a bigger mistake, and to be hugely kind to ourselves when we make one of those giant, ugly, and embarrassing mistakes.

It takes superpowers to trust that we will recover and learn from these mistakes and that maybe they aren't mistakes at all.

Kindness. Trust. Choice. Just three of the many simple words that have the power to change our lives and to impact the lives of the people around us.

Interestingly, these powers only work when we are not wearing a disguise or hiding behind a mask. They only work when we show up as ourselves. And, on the days we aren't able to access these powers, and we all have those days, we must simply do the best we can.

## *Ask yourself:*

- What are my superpowers?

- What are three simple, yet powerful, words that resonate with me, and why?

- What mistakes have I made that have turned out not to be mistakes at all?

# Waking Up Sleeping Beauty

Lately, I've become fascinated with Sleeping Beauty, the fairytale about a lovely princess who, when she turned fifteen years old, pricked her finger on a spindle and fell asleep for 100 years. Pretty boring, right?

When the princess was born, the king and queen had a large celebration, and all the kingdom was invited, including the fairies. Each fairy brought the baby a special gift. The gifts she was given were beauty, wit, grace, and virtue, as well as the gifts of music and dance.

Before the last gift was offered, a fairy who hadn't been seen for many, many years suddenly appeared—and I believe her words have been misinterpreted over the centuries.

With a look of tremendous sadness and grief, she proclaimed, "If these are the only gifts this little girl is given, she will certainly die by her fifteenth birthday, for no one thought to offer her gifts of courage and strength, of adventure and purpose, of self-worth." Then this forgotten fairy turned and vanished as suddenly as she had appeared.

Everyone was horrified. Fortunately, there was one fairy who had a final gift to offer. Not a sound was heard when the remaining fairy spoke. "This precious child will not die, but sleep for one hundred years and will be awakened by her true love."

Reading this fairytale, I wondered where our gifts really do come from. Are they given to us by others? Sometimes. Are we able to choose our own gifts? Certainly. Are they within each of us, patiently waiting to be discovered? Absolutely.

When we become disconnected from any of our gifts, it's easy to feel as if we have been asleep for 100 years. For certainly, these gifts are waiting within each us to be discovered, to be examined, to be celebrated.

And, when we learn to love ourselves, we will always awaken.

*Ask yourself:*

- Which special gifts were given to me, and which did I discover myself?

- What gifts am I still searching for?

- How can I tell that I'm "waking up"?

# The "Be Mine" Candy Heart

When Valentine's Day is approaching, it can feel like an unwelcome neighbor whose arms are filled with greeting cards covered in red hearts and sugary sentiments professing love.

We cringe because this holiday seems dedicated to celebrating everything we have lost or possibly never had.

Still, we can dream.

We may imagine a new Valentine will come along with reservations for an intimate candlelight dinner, bringing us red roses and chocolates.

However, we may also be thrilled if someone simply appears at our door with a pint of Hot Fudge Ripple ice cream and a soup spoon and entertains us by cleaning the house and doing all the laundry.

Sadly, for those of us who have felt so terribly alone during our past relationships, expecting anything from a partner seems like a wasted effort. The price we had paid to be in these relationships was too dear. Like the lyrics of a romantic song, we had "lost our hearts," but not in a good way.

Then I saw the message "Be Mine" stamped on a Valentine's Day candy heart. I used to think this meant that someone else wanted me to be theirs. I was wrong. It meant that I can "Be Mine."

Ah, "Be Mine." It sounded wonderful; however, during my marriage, I felt like I had disappeared. So, in order to "Be Mine," I had to find myself and rediscover who I was. During this process, I realized that my self-esteem would no longer depend on a relationship with another and that meeting a potential new Valentine would no longer cause me to frantically ask myself, "Will he like me? I hope he likes me! What if he doesn't like me?" Instead, I now take a breath and ask myself, "Hmm, I wonder if I'll like him?"

Now that is sweet!

## Ask yourself:

- How do I answer the question, "Who am I"?

- What does it mean to be my own Valentine?

- How will being my own Valentine affect any future relationships?

# Expect a "Visit"

The day finally came when my divorce, and the worst of its pain, was over. I was in great emotional shape. Well, maybe not great, but darn good. Stopping at the grocery store early one evening, I turned down the frozen food aisle and there, right in front of me, was a man wearing the same jacket my ex-husband often wore.

My heart started to pound. I broke into a sweat and felt myself suddenly tumbling back down into a familiar dark hole. The grief I thought had passed came roaring back, almost knocking me off my feet. I grabbed a frozen pizza, abruptly turned my shopping cart around and, of course, got into the slowest checkout line in the store.

The following afternoon, I went horseback riding with a friend. Being around horses is comforting for me, and a quiet trail ride with someone I trusted was just what I needed. As our horses calmly walked side by side, I shared my grocery store experience, admitting that it felt like I had failed in some way and needed to go through the exhausting healing process all over again.

My friend, divorced for many years, said, "Oh, you've had a 'visit.' I would get them too. It's a normal reaction whenever a painful memory is triggered, and the trigger can be as simple as a song, a picture, or even a jacket. Don't worry. You don't have to start anything over again. Healing just takes a lot more time than we expect."

I let out a sigh of relief, and for the first time that afternoon, I felt the warmth of the sun and noticed the beauty of the open sky.

I would remember to be patient, knowing that as time passed, the "visits" would fade, and there was always a world of possibilities around me as wide and open as the sky.

## Ask yourself:

- What experiences or situations do, or could, cause a "visit"?

- How can I prepare myself for a "visit"?

- What can I do to comfort myself after a "visit"?

# Be Honest with Yourself

At one point, I had decided to follow the often-repeated advice, "Fake it until you make it."

I tried to fake confidence and ignore the voice in my head, insisting that I was a terrible mother, a terrible money manager, a terrible friend, a terrible everything. To silence that voice, I watched TV marathon reruns of *Law & Order*, *Will & Grace*, and *CSI*.

I tried to fake strength and ignore the voice insisting that I was a victim and that kept moaning, "Poor me, poor me. I've been betrayed, abused, cheated on." To silence it, I went to the refrigerator and ate leftovers from my favorite local Chinese restaurant and Hot Fudge Ripple ice cream from a carton I found in the back of the freezer.

Eventually, the voices began to bore me, and I actually had the audacity to doubt them. When my stomach couldn't take much more, and my mind was sufficiently numbed by the TV, it became clear that if I "faked it," I would never "make it." So I tried honesty.

My first thought was, *I'm honestly screwed!* But that wasn't the truth—not even close. The truth, which took a while longer to discover and to admit, was that I was stronger and more powerful than I realized. I decided to plant myself in the messy soil of my life and trust I would grow and blossom.

## Ask yourself:

- What am I discovering as I become more honest with myself?

- How does it feel when I'm in my personal power?

- What is the "messy soil of my life," and how will I begin to plant myself in it?

# Who Am I Without All My Stuff?

I had already lost so much that was intangible in my life, including the love of a partner who I thought was my best friend, my dreams for the future, as well as my memories of the past that turned out to be a lie.

I had lost the path I'd been on for so long. Some days it felt like I was wandering in a dark forest without a sense of direction. Other days it felt as if I was floating alone in a vast ocean without oars, a map, and certainly without an anchor.

As shallow as this makes me sound, sometimes these issues were so overwhelming, it was easier for me to focus on stuff.

I did not lose all my stuff during my divorce, but I lost enough to make me realize how much of my life was defined by it—and how much I defined myself by it. At first, I was frightened, then angry, then blaming, and finally embarrassed. "Why can't I recognize myself without my stuff?"

And I had a bigger problem. I believed people judged me by my choice of stuff, so I needed to have stuff they would like, too, and think was really cool. But now, with so much of my stuff gone, what would happen to me?

"Time to grow up, Sweetie!" I whispered to myself.

Stuff is fun and can bring joy and beauty into our lives, but it does not define any of us. We have the privilege of doing that ourselves. Stuff is not a substitute for meaning, purpose, or fulfillment. Often, the stuff that we do treasure is quite simple and can be found in unexpected places. I have a rock collection I love. This collection grew because I was simply looking where I was going.

Where are you going? What stuff will you choose to leave behind, and what will you keep and treasure?

## Ask yourself:

- How and why have I allowed stuff to define me?

- What stuff do I treasure and why?

- How am I defining myself without my stuff?

# Finding Your Voice

Joining the ranks of other divorced and divorcing women, I came to the painful realization that during my marriage, I had lost my voice, and with it, the ability to speak my truth. I hoped that finding my voice would be like finding my car keys at the bottom of my purse or the sunglasses I had forgotten were actually on top of my head.

I was wrong. After searching outside of myself, I realized that my voice wasn't lost—it was hidden. I had buried it deep in my heart to protect it from being battered and attacked.

I had buried it so deeply that at first I could only hear it whisper to me, and in all the commotion of daily life, eventually, I heard nothing. I sensed I'd lost touch with something vital...but could not remember what it was.

When we lose our voice, our spirit fades. We feel unsettled and anxious. Believing we are powerless, we stop trusting ourselves. Some of us become depressed and resentful, or look to other people or material things to define us, or all of the above and more.

To excavate our precious voice takes courage. I had always believed that if I spoke my truth, I would be abandoned. I had forgotten that someone who truly loved me would listen to me with respect. I realized that by silencing my voice, I was the one who abandoned myself.

Determined never to let this happen again, I began to listen carefully for those whispers. The more I listened, the stronger the voice became, and soon I found the courage to act on what I heard.

Maybe finding our voice is like finding our car keys and sunglasses. We can get behind the wheel of life, protect our eyes from any harsh glare, and start down a new road singing our favorite song.

## Ask yourself:

- What were some of the things I didn't say that I wish I had, and what do I think would have happened if I did?

- How have my adult dreams changed as a result of my divorce?

- How can I begin to realize these dreams when I am ready?

# Dreaming Girl

When I was first married, my husband and I bought an artist's print of a young girl sitting with her legs pulled up, so her chin rested on her knees, and her arms gently wrapped around her legs. The artist named the print "Dreaming Girl," because he surrounded her with pieces of her dream: images of a bird, a sea shell, a pink-and-yellow butterfly, and a tree with sun shining through its branches. Scattered around her, he painted pastel-colored stones and a soft-blue feather.

I loved this picture from the first moment I saw it, because it gave me a sense of peace.

Years later, when my divorce process began, my attitude towards this picture changed. I wanted to shout at this girl, "Look up! Get up! Do something! Terrible things will happen if you don't pay attention to what is going on in your life." I now considered her extremely irresponsible and had absolutely no patience for her.

Time passed. The divorce was finalized, and life went on. Throughout all the trauma and drama, the girl in the picture had never wavered from what she had been created to do...which was to dream.

When we are struggling and feel certain we will never dream again, the girl within each of us waits patiently, for we, too, have been created to dream—and when we do, life opens up for us in simple, beautiful, and unexpected ways.

## *Ask yourself:*

- What were my little girl dreams?

- How have my adult dreams changed as a result of my divorce?

- How can I begin to realize these new dreams when I am ready?

# Do We Have Self-Esteem Backwards?

I had always believed that even if my self-esteem wasn't that good, at least it was adequate, although there were days during my divorce when I found it curled up in a ball in the corner of the bathroom and feared it would never recover. When it did recover, I thought that proved I was now capable of handling just about anything

But it turns out that whenever I have to face a new challenge and life expects me to be something more than I think I am, I freeze.

I hope that if I ignore the situation, it will go away. I remind myself of my cats who think if they don't look at something, it's not there.

When I finally do look at this new "challenge" (sometimes I really don't like this word!), my first reaction is, "I can't handle this." And then I watch a TV episode of *Judge*

*Judy* so I can feel superior to both the plaintiff and the defendant who have each made a mess of their lives.

Eventually, I remember my love of horses and how it led me to take riding lessons and compete. It was many years ago, but the lessons I learned have continued to guide me.

At first, I was embarrassed by how poorly I rode, but there was always someone who picked me up and dusted me off, often literally. My riding coach told me that it's the mistakes we make that teach us the most, which was lucky for me because I made lots of them.

Not only did these mistakes teach me how to become a better rider, but they also taught me that I would survive being embarrassed and that my mistakes did not define me any more than my blue ribbons did—causing my self-esteem to no longer be dependent on what I could or couldn't achieve.

I believe self-esteem...
- does not come from reading motivational books, though they do help.
- does not come from meditation, though it does help.
- does come from walking out the door and living your life.

With each step, and each misstep, you learn not only more about yourself, you realize that we are all doing the best we can.

Life is filled with confusion and joy, messes and celebrations, mistakes and miracles. What could be better?

## *Ask yourself:*

- What valuable lessons have I learned from my mistakes?

- Where does my self-esteem come from if it's not from my achievements?

- What is helping me heal and strengthen my self-esteem?

# Rent or Own My Life?

At the beginning of my divorce, I moved into an apartment until I was able to purchase a townhouse, which was the first time I'd ever had a mortgage in my own name. I was very excited and a little scared. During my first summer in the townhouse, I noticed the front screen door was no longer hanging correctly in its frame. The refrigerator began making strange sounds, and every time I heard it shudder, I sent out a prayer that it keep working—the same with my garbage disposal. Then I had to use the flashlight on my cell phone to go up the steps to my bedroom at night because the hallway light burned out, and I couldn't reach the ceiling fixture to change the bulb and didn't have a ladder I trusted.

Frustrated with my fix-it to-do list, I thought, *If I was renting, I wouldn't have to deal with all these things, and life would be so much easier.*

Then I wondered if I could do that with my life...just rent instead of own. Someone else could fix everything that was broken and also take care of all the messy stuff: financial issues, stress issues, emotional issues.

Wow! Now that would certainly make things easy. But then it wouldn't be my life. I would no longer have a sense of who I was, and would rely on advertisers and other media to tell me how I should look, and how "spring fresh" my house should smell. I might forget to look into my heart when deciding moral and ethical issues and instead depend on the loudest, most bullying voices to tell me what to think, and what was fake and what was real.

Owning our lives can be messy and uncertain at times, but it is a privilege, a gift. With guidance, support, and the love of others, it can also be exhilarating, joyful, and thrilling. The tapestry of every life is woven with colors that are both brilliant and dark, with experiences that both lift us up and cause us to stumble. This is how we learn to be resilient, compassionate, and courageous. This is how we learn who we truly are. I decided I do not want to become a stranger to myself—thus, renting is not an option.

As for my townhouse, I called a handyman.

## Ask yourself:

- What emotions come up when I acknowledge that I "own my life"?
- What are the biggest issues I'm facing as I "own my life," and how are they impacting my choices and my dreams?
- Which experiences have caused me to stumble, and which have lifted me up?

# What Does Healing Really Look Like?

Coffee with a friend can be filled with unexpected conversations. Over her latte and my mint tea, Cynthia shared that she was very disappointed in herself, and I couldn't imagine why.

Then she shared that a few weeks earlier, she and her sister, Kelly, were waiting to be seated at a restaurant when she happened to turn around and suddenly found herself face-to-face with her ex—and she froze.

She didn't remember what she said or if she even said anything. She simply shut down, and Kelly gently took her arm, guiding her as the hostess led them to their table.

Once they were seated, Cynthia started to shake. "What just happened to me? The divorce was over ten years ago. I've worked so hard to heal. I don't understand. Am I falling back down into that awful dark hole? I'm terrified of going through the pain it will take to climb back out again."

"No, you haven't fallen down any dark hole, and no, you don't have to climb back out of anything," Kelly reassured her. "Your body instinctively sensed danger, and that triggered its fight-flight-freeze response. It's as simple as that, and of the three, I'm grateful you chose freeze. If you had decided to flee, you're pretty fast. I wouldn't have been able to catch up with you, and a fight would have been just plain messy!"

Cynthia giggled when she shared her sister's words with me. Then she sighed and confessed that she assumed once she had healed, she would simply move on. But our bodies have long memories, and sometimes it takes more time than we realize to reassure ourselves we are safe.

We decided healing isn't a package with a bow that you receive as a reward for the hard work you have done. We didn't want to imagine healing as that smelly onion with all the layers that you keep peeling off while it makes your eyes water.

We agreed that healing was an adventure, an exploration. Whether the new scenery we encounter is dark and frightening or shimmering with light, it would constantly challenge our perspectives, and sometimes even take our breath away.

*Ask yourself:*

- How does my body protect me when it feels my stress?

- What does healing feel like or look like to me?

- As I heal, how is my perspective shifting, and what, if any, new scenery do I notice?

# Self-Love...You're Kidding, Right?

I hadn't even heard the phrase "self-love" until I was in my forties. It seemed way too sappy a concept and too overwhelming a request, but I had decided to give it a try and was surprised and truly flattered when a respected life coach asked to interview me on the topic. She explained that the interview would be videotaped, and I went to work compiling as much information as I could and doing another round of self-reflection, as well. (I can only handle so much self-reflection at a time.)

During the interview, I explained that in the past my focus had always been outward, doing my best to make sure others loved me. I shared that my journey to self-love began when a trauma forced me down into my heart, shifting my focus inward. Love seemed to be too big a step to take at the beginning of this new relationship, so I had begun by simply being a friend to myself. I began to speak my truth...most of the time, and to be gentle with myself... some of the time.

When the video ended, the first words out of my mouth were, "My hair looked terrible! I used my hands too much! I talked too fast! I sounded awful!"

The life coach who had interviewed me couldn't stop laughing. "Are you listening to what you are saying? Didn't you just spend an hour talking about self-love?"

I laughed too. I was so busted. Was I a fraud? Is it possible to be a star-crossed lover with yourself, almost connecting but not quite? Nah, I was simply human.

I now have a simple three-step approach to self-love:
1. Practice.
2. Make lots of mistakes.
3. Laugh as often you can.

To navigate the divorce process, we obviously need to focus outward. Yet divorce can be the trauma that forces us down into our broken hearts to heal them...and what heals our hearts is self-love.

*Ask yourself:*

- What steps can I take to become more of a friend to myself?

- What does self-love mean to me?

- What makes me laugh?

# You're Confused? Hooray!

Lately, I've been quite confused. It's not the usual confusion of wondering why I walked into a room or where I put my car keys when I'm holding them. What's confusing is I've not been myself lately. I've been feeling out of sorts. It's like I'm not able to get traction in my life.

When I shared my feelings with a friend, she clapped her hands together and said, "Hooray! That's wonderful!"

"What? Why in the world would you say that?"

"It's simple. You've been working hard to discard your limiting beliefs, and now you no longer fit the image you've had of yourself, and that can be tremendously confusing. But as a result, you're growing into something new and expanded, and that's truly a reason to celebrate."

The more I thought about her words, the more comforted I became. Aren't we all doing our best to learn and grow? Wouldn't it make sense that the more we discover, the more we will reevaluate our beliefs and discard those that no longer serve us?

As we begin to redefine ourselves with less judgment and more compassion, we can clarify our purpose and how we choose to journey through life.

May we each continue to learn and grow, and when we experience times of confusion, let's celebrate!

*Ask yourself:*

- What am I the most confused about?

- What limiting beliefs have I discarded?

- Which of my beliefs are even more precious to me, and why?

# It's Not That Bad

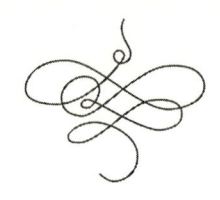

One Saturday, I hurt my back with a simple twist as I was standing up. On Sunday, even though my back ached and was very tender, I went for a short, careful walk. It was a beautiful day, and as I shuffled around the neighborhood, passing yards planted with fresh spring flowers, I wondered why I was surprised to be in pain.

I knew my posture at the computer was not good. I knew reading in bed caused me to slouch even more than being at the computer. I knew the chair I liked to sit in at the end of the day, so the cat could curl up on my lap, was a terrible fit for my body.

So, if I knew all these things, why hadn't I done something about them?

I have a feeling I'm not the only one who waits, thinking things really aren't that bad, that I can handle being uncomfortable, that it's not a big deal, and anyway, I've gotten used to it.

Of course, I can handle being uncomfortable, but why wouldn't I change the situation if I could? Why should I get used to it if I don't have to? Do I think it's going to help me build character?

One sign of character is the willingness to respect and care for myself as well as others. This willingness to respect and care for myself is also a reflection of self-worth, and I was disheartened to discover that after all these years, I still struggle with this issue.

Walking past another lovely garden, I understood that my self-worth is not yet a perennial that returns and blossoms year after year. Instead, it needs to be planted anew every season.

### Ask yourself:

- What in my life doesn't fit, or causes physical or emotional pain?
- Why have I been waiting to change these things?
- What do I believe builds character?

# Being at Ease in Your Own Life

I recently had my townhouse's furnace ducts cleaned. For some reason, this motivated me to clean the shelf in my kitchen where I dump everything that I don't know what to do with. Then I began to clean out a drawer here and a closet there.

When I started cleaning my oven, I began to worry. I couldn't even remember the last time I'd done this and wondered what in the world had come over me.

Was there something deeper, more vital, that I was really trying to clean?

Wouldn't it be nice to just vacuum up self-doubt or scrub away fear? How about cleaning out the drawer where I stash all my anger and frustration to pretend they're gone?

A perfectly clean home or a perfectly clean attitude need not—and I believe should not—be expected of any of us. Life is messy. Emotions are messy. We are going to spill coffee on the rug. We are going to have those little dribbles of toothpaste in the bathroom sink. Sometimes our fear is going to spill onto our faith, and sometimes our doubt is going to dribble all over our confidence.

Most of us clean our house on a regular basis, or at least once in a while. It's wise of us to do the same with our emotions.

My hope is that this work will deepen our relationship with ourselves and allow us to become more at ease in our own lives.

*Ask yourself:*

- How do I react when fear spills onto my faith?
- How do I react when doubt affects my confidence?
- How can I become at ease in my own life?

# Release

In my office is a picture I cut out of a magazine many years ago. It is a photograph of a horse in mid-flight over a very large jump. The horse is being ridden by a young woman, and in large red letters at the top of the picture is the word "Release."

The article that accompanied the picture explained that if you don't release the reins, the horse cannot jump—and it will not be able to get over the hurdle that's in front of it. Sure enough, in the picture, the young woman's hands are resting partway up her horse's neck, and there is a big loop in her reins.

Looking at the picture, you frantically ask yourself, "How can she do that? Isn't she afraid? What if something happens? How does she stay on?"

There are two answers:

First is her focus. She is not looking down. She is not looking behind her. She is not looking at the people in the viewing stands. She is looking forward.

Second, her power and security does not come from holding the reins. That is only an illusion. Her security comes from the strength in her legs and in her core.

The picture is a constant reminder that tightly holding onto something will not protect me, and there are issues I must deal with and release if I want to move forward in my life.

We each have that list of what we want to release, and when we understand that our strength comes from the core of who we are, we will be able to look forward with confidence, knowing we have the ability to overcome any obstacles in our path.

*Ask yourself:*

- What are the major hurdles in front of me that I want to get over?

- What illusions am I holding on to, and how can I feel safe releasing them?

- What are the core strengths and values that keep me secure?

# Forgiveness and Fishing

One evening I was listening to a conversation on forgiveness when a woman said, "If I forgive my ex, it's like I'm letting him off the hook—and there is no way he should be let off the hook!"

I thought about her comment all night and realized that many of us feel this way, especially if we want our ex to be held accountable for unethical or cruel behavior. Yet, we need to be aware that sometimes accountability will happen, and sometimes it won't, and even if it does, we may never be aware of it.

I imagine a woman sitting at the end of a dock with her fishing pole. The fishing line is in the water. She feels certain that a fish is biting on the hook at the end of the line, though that might only be her imagination, and if it was there for a moment, it may have already swum away.

Forgiveness is not about taking your ex (or a fish) off the hook. But, when we are ready, it's about setting down the fishing pole and going to lunch.

Though we might return several times to that dock and pick up that pole, we no longer need to hold on to it for very long, for we have felt the freedom that comes from setting it down.

### *Ask yourself:*

- What am I struggling with the most when it comes to forgiveness?

- What will it take, or what has it taken, for me to let my ex, or myself, off the hook?

- What would, or does, forgiveness feel like in my mind, heart, and spirit?

# Finding Peace Within

*May today there be peace within.
May you trust God that you are exactly
where you are meant to be.
May you not forget the infinite possibilities
that are born of faith.
May you use those gifts that you have received,
and pass on the love that has been given to you.
May you be content knowing you are a child of God.
Let this presence settle into your bones, and allow
your soul the freedom to sing, dance, praise and love.
It is there for each and every one of us.*

—Saint Teresa of Avila
(1515–1582)

I love this, but it does seem to gloss over a few things. It's easy to find "peace within" when your life is calm, but not when it is in chaos.

It's easy to "trust that you are exactly where you are meant to be" when you're in a place you enjoy, but not when the foundation of your life feels as if it's crumbling under your feet.

And, being content can be a constant challenge.

Then there is her last sentence: "It is there for each and every one of us." I want so badly for this to be true, but many women, especially during divorce, have forgotten how to access these lovely concepts. Some fiercely doubt them altogether, and others feel sorrow that they're so out of reach.

It would have been helpful if St. Teresa had given us directions to these places of peace, trust, and contentment. She could have left a treasure map with an X to mark the spot or directions for "easy assembly" like those that come with small pieces of furniture that have to be put together.

But X does not always mark the spot, and assembly directions always leave you with extra pieces, so you worry that what you've put together will not hold.

I believe she did not give us directions because we are each on our own journey. There are times we will take a step forward and times we will be still. In times of stillness, we will recognize that peace, trust, and contentment have been with us always, unseen or forgotten in the challenges and chaos of our lives.

It turns out Saint Teresa did not gloss over anything. She left a beautiful reminder of the treasures we have within us, none of which need any assembly.

## *Ask yourself:*

- How can I find peace in the midst of the chaos of divorce and the life changes it creates?

- What does the word "faith" mean to me?

- What is helping me trust that I'm exactly where I'm meant to be?

# Reflections of the Season

And, when we learn to love ourselves, we will always awaken.

There was always a world of possibilities around me as wide and open as the sky.

I decided to plant myself in the messy soil of my life and trust I would grow and blossom.

Maybe finding our voice is like finding our car keys and sunglasses. We can get behind the wheel of life, protect our eyes from any harsh glare, and start down a new road singing our favorite song.

The girl within each of us waits patiently, for we, too, have been created to dream.

*Life will be filled with confusion and joy, messes and celebrations, mistakes and miracles. What could be better?*

*I decided I do not want to become a stranger to myself.*

*We agreed that healing is an adventure, an exploration....it would constantly challenge us and sometimes even take our breath away.*

*Forgiveness is not about taking your ex (or a fish) off the hook. But, when we are ready, it's about setting down the fishing pole and going to lunch.*

*In times of stillness, we will recognize that peace, trust, and contentment have been with us always.*

# Summer

# Butterfly Sightings

One summer, when I was a little girl, maybe six or seven years old, my mother bought me a butterfly net to keep me busy and out of the house. It was a wise decision. I spent hours running across our lawn, chasing beautiful monarch butterflies, wildly swinging my net, and gratefully never catching anything. Then I would collapse on the soft grass and look up at the sky.

Many decades later, on a walk around my neighborhood, a monarch butterfly floated by, landing on a lovely yellow flower. Though I no longer chase butterflies, they always make me stop and smile.

When I was young, I did not understand how hard butterflies had to fight to break free of their cocoons. I did not understand that this struggle to break free built their strength, and it was this struggle that saved them.

My recent butterfly sighting reminded me to honor the struggles that saved me and gave me the strength to find my way to this new life.

It reminded me to see the possibilities of my future and find joy in my journey. These possibilities cannot be captured by wildly swinging a net. They can only be discovered when we let our dreams and our imaginations float free and show us the way.

*Ask yourself:*

- What images or memories do butterflies bring up for me?

- What was the "cocoon" from which I needed to break free?

- In what way has the struggle of my divorce saved me?

# Tubing Down the River

I was recently on vacation in Colorado with my children and grandchildren. One morning we all decided to go tubing down a section of the San Juan River, which I thought would be the same as tubing down the gentle Apple River close to home. Well, I was mistaken!

Even though the water level was low, I overturned on the second small set of rapids, and when I popped up from the water, my tube was swiftly floating away from me. The water was shallow enough for me to walk towards my tube, but I couldn't keep my footing on the slippery rocks in the river bed and kept falling back into the icy cold river. I was very grateful when my younger daughter grabbed the tube and held it for me until I could climb back in.

I decided to float closer to the shoreline where the water was calm, assuming I would be safer, but the only thing that happened was I got stuck in the shallows. I had simply exchanged one set of problems for another.

With my legs dangling over the edge of my tube, I began to maneuver my way back into the flow of the river. My older daughter was floating by, and seeing me struggling, she reached out, grabbed ahold of my ankle, and held onto me until we reached our downriver destination, which felt like hours but probably took only twenty minutes.

Looking back up the river from where we had come, the rapids seemed so small, and I wondered why they had frightened me so terribly. It was interesting that of all the wonderful, heartwarming memories of this family vacation, my mind kept returning to this experience. It was embarrassing. It was funny. And it was chock-full of metaphors.

Divorce certainly tosses us out of the safety of our lives and leave us feeling stranded in an icy new reality.

We see our security float away, and we can't keep our footing in order to catch it. We may want to stay close to what feels safe, but we have to be careful not to get stuck away from the flow of the river, the flow of life.

We all need someone to reach out and hold and support us so we can navigate the frightening turbulence of this difficult time.

We can be compassionate with ourselves when we look back from where we have come and we can gaze at new scenery in our lives and search for meaning.

## *Ask yourself:*

- When during my divorce have I lost my footing, and how have I, or can I, regain it?

- Where have I gotten stuck trying to stay safe?

- How has the support of others holding onto me made a difference, and what has that taught me?

# Taking off the Training Wheels

One day I witnessed a wonderful scene in our neighborhood. The training wheels were off—and the three little girls were pedaling furiously, and for the moment, all three bikes were staying upright. What excitement!

Steering was now a challenge. The bikes wiggled and looped shakily back and forth across the quiet road, and staying upright does not always last very long when you are learning something new.

Sometimes a bike tipped over, dropping its rider on the soft grass of a neighbor's lawn, and a little girl needed help getting her bike upright once again.

Sometimes a bike stalled in a driveway, which also happens when you are learning something new, and a little girl needed a push to get moving once more.

The little girls didn't stop because they weren't doing things right. They didn't complain that it was hard, for it certainly was. They didn't think about being perfect, but eagerly started again every time they stopped, or their bike tipped over. These girls only heard voices of encouragement. "You can do it! Try again! Wonderful! You've got this!"

As adults, it often seems we're more likely to hear the voices that insist, "Why do you think you can do this? You're not coordinated. You'll never stay upright. You're going to be so embarrassed when you fall down."

This may be why we don't want to take the training wheels off our life. We want to cling to things that make us feel secure and seem to keep us steady, whether they be situations, relationships, attitudes, or unexamined beliefs. Yet these may be the same things that keep us from moving forward and experiencing more of life and the joy it holds. To honor every little girl so she can grow strong and confident, and to honor the little girl within each us, let's choose carefully which voices we listen to.

Life can sometimes certainly feel shaky. Let's ask for help when we need a push, and let's remember, "We've got this!"

## Ask yourself:

- In what areas of my life am I ready to take off the "training wheels" and why?

- In what areas of my life do I feel I still need "training wheels" and why?

- What were the most memorable times I "fell," and what gave me the courage to get up and start again?

# Enjoy Looking Up

Friday afternoon, I was at a stoplight, waiting for the green arrow that would give me permission to take a left turn into the grocery store parking lot. Out of the corner of my eye, I noticed what I thought was a large bird begin to circle low in the sky. The light changed, I pulled into the lot, parked, and got out of my car.

Standing against the car door, I looked up once again, curious. The bird was still circling, and I realized it was a white-headed bald eagle. All I could think of was, *Wow!*

I watched, enthralled, as he gracefully flapped his powerful wings once or twice and then glided on the air currents. He seemed to be having a wonderful time playing with the sky. After a few minutes, he began circling higher and higher, eventually disappearing into the clouds.

It felt as if he wanted to make sure I saw him, and once I did, he went on his way, and I sent him a prayer of gratitude.

When my focus returned to the parking lot, I realized no one else had looked up. There was grace and beauty and joy right above us, and no one noticed. I was about to ask myself, "How does that happen?" but I knew all too well how that happens.

We live with the anxious rush of life, the pressures of to-do lists, and goals and expectations that can drive us to distraction.

Then there are times when we become weighed down by life circumstances, by pain and grief, and it takes too much effort to lift our heads, which was what happened to me during my divorce, and for a long time afterwards. The days when I did make the effort to look up, I saw nothing so I stopped looking.

How do we remind ourselves to look up—or find the courage to look again?

It may be to simply stay open to the possibilities of beauty and grace and joy, believing we can find them anywhere, even on a chilly day in a grocery store parking lot in the middle of the city.

## *Ask yourself:*

- What new ways am I learning to handle the pressures of life?

- How can I remind myself to look up?

- When I do look up, what do I see?

# Untangling Truth from Fear

On a walk around the neighborhood, I came upon two rabbits playing with each other near a large evergreen. At first, they didn't notice me. Then one stood very still, flicked his ears, and took off with his playmate following quickly behind him. They both disappeared into the shadows of the welcoming tree.

In some cultures, rabbits are a reminder to be discerning about what to fear and what not to fear. Continuing on my walk, I acknowledged that I had a very, very long list of fears. If being afraid were an Olympic sport, I would be a champion.

That night, I read a quote by author David R. Hawkins: "Our fears have been based on falsehood. Displacement of the false by the truth is the essence of healing all things visible and invisible."

I have been certain my fears are the truth. I've been certain I'm not competent. I've been certain I'm a fraud. I've been certain I'm not worthy of what the world wants to offer me.

My fear has become entwined with my truth, like two necklaces on a dresser that have become tangled together, and the lovely patterns and sparkling gems of my truth have become harder to see, almost invisible.

I know from experience that to separate the necklaces I have to sit calmly and carefully find where the two separate chains have become twisted together before I can disconnect one from the other. Sometimes I figure it out quickly, and other times, not so much.

When this is done, each can have its own place on my dresser, and I can choose which one I will wear.

## Ask yourself:

- On what falsehoods have I based my fears?

- How did my truths and fears become so tangled together?

- As I untangle my fears, what truths can I see more clearly?

# INDEPENDENCE DAY

With the Fourth of July coming fast, I thought about the strong, independent women I wanted to emulate and to be my role models. Unfortunately, the first image that came to me was Wonder Woman standing with her hands on her hips, staring out at the world with confidence and strength and, of course, looking great.

Then my mind screamed, *Stop!* I know a lot of amazing, strong women, and none of them look like that, and I would be very nervous if they did.

I realized it's not being independent that makes these women so strong. It is being dependent that gives them strength. They are dependent on great friends and mentors who support, guide, and encourage them. They are dependent on their connection to something larger than themselves, a Higher Power, by whatever name they choose to call that source of love and compassion and healing. They are dependent on laughter and tears and hope for the future, even in the darkest of times.

I was told that the root system of the giant, majestic redwood tree does not go very deep into the earth. Instead, the roots intertwine with each other. And being interconnected is the reason they are able to grow strong, powerful, and beautiful.

We may worry about being dependent because sometimes what people depend on can be unhealthy, dangerous, or smacks of addiction of some sort. But when we choose wisely to depend on things that bring light into our lives, the possibilities for our future are unlimited.

## Ask yourself:

- What people, beliefs, or experiences do I depend on the most that give me strength?

- Is there anything I depend on that is not healthy, and if so, how can I change this?

- What does being independent mean to me?

# County Fair

One Friday night in August, I went to the local county fair with three women friends who were all divorced. Life after divorce can really be an adventure, and we were quite a group. One of us had trouble walking, one had trouble hearing, and I had trouble staying awake. Luckily the youngest was in great shape and kept us moving.

We ate. We looked at horses, cows, goats, and sheep. We ate. We looked at beautiful flower arrangements and intricately designed quilts. We ate...and we laughed and laughed.

Women always hear about self-care, especially during divorce. We are instructed to eat well, exercise, get enough sleep, and keep our attitudes positive so we can move forward.

There seems to be such a rush to move forward, and sometimes it simply seems like too much work.

Instead of moving forward, Friday felt like we were going back in time, remembering fairs we attended when we were young, how we loved horses, and how we used to be able to eat so much more before our stomachs complained.

Walking back to the car at the end of this August night, I felt calmer, more hopeful, and more light-hearted than I had in quite a while.

During my divorce, joy had seemed so very far away.

I did lose touch with women who I thought were friends but who felt they had to choose sides and did not choose me. Now extraordinary new friends have appeared. Their presence gives me energy, confidence, and courage.

Friendship heals. It comforts. It is precious medicine for the soul.

*Ask yourself:*

- What past memories bring me joy?
- How can I bring joy into the present?
- What gifts have my friendships provided me?

# Healing on a Stick?

After the Minnesota State Fair has ended, if we are craving any more treats on a stick, we have to wait for another year. We have to be content imagining that extraordinary culinary creation in our hands, taking that first bite, sighing contently, and knowing nothing can be all that bad when you're eating something so special.

I found a mouthwatering list of seventy-five foods you can get on a stick, including frozen coffee, chocolate-covered cheesecake, deep-fried candy bars, spaghetti and meatballs, and even a Texas steak dinner. I had no idea!

To successfully eat anything on a stick, it's important to concentrate on what you are holding, so whatever is on the stick doesn't fall off and slide down the front of your shirt, or drip in a sticky mess through your fingers. It's often helpful to sit for a while on a nearby bench to better focus on the treat in front of you.

When you feel you have nibbled this treat down to a manageable amount, you may decide to get off the bench and rejoin the colorful, vibrant flow of life. That is a wonderful decision, but you still need to pay attention to what is in your hand, and in doing so, you may find yourself somewhere unexpected, wondering how in the world you ended up behind the horse barn or in the middle of Machinery Hill.

What would it be like, I wondered, if you could walk up to a vendor and order healing on a stick? It might seem like such a big serving, more than you could manage, but it would have colored sprinkles of peace and joy to make you smile.

What would it be like to sit and concentrate on your healing, taking one bite at a time? Sometimes it might be messy and sticky, and you might drop parts of it down the front of your shirt. But you would keep nibbling and eventually re-enter the flow of life. You would still need to pay attention, or you could find yourself in unexpected places: some upsetting, some thrilling, most comforting.

When you have finished your serving of healing on a stick, you would realize you have gained peace, not pounds, and the healing was so sweet, you might even ask for another serving.

### *Ask yourself:*

- What are the ingredients in my healing on a stick?

- What parts of my healing on a stick are the messiest and stickiest, and why?

- What can I do when I find myself not quite healed and a little lost?

# I'm So Proud of Myself

My eight-year-old granddaughter was in the cast of the show, *Honk!* a musical based on the story "The Ugly Duckling."

Sitting in the middle school auditorium on opening night, my daughter and I grinned and grinned every time we saw her on stage. In two scenes she was one of the little kitties scampering around, and in a third she was one of the frogs that hopped and danced during the number, "Warts and All!"

At the end of the show, the performers took their bows and then came into the auditorium to find their families and get hugs. With her little kitty ears still on her head, she smiled brightly and said to us, "I'm so proud of myself!"

Her joyful, spontaneous statement took my breath away.

It's always been so hard for me to say those words. In

fact, I can't remember the last time I did, and I can always undermine any sense of pride by making lists of all the things I did wrong in any situation.

Maybe I never learned that I don't have to be perfect to feel proud of what I have done.

Maybe I always thought I would sound conceited if I shared how I felt, though it never sounds that way when it comes from your heart.

Maybe I wanted to stay small because it felt safer not to be noticed.

I find it so interesting that we have learned to honor our feelings of grief, sadness, and depression, but many of us have forgotten to honor our feelings of pride.

It takes courage to feel proud. It takes honesty. It takes practice.

When we can feel proud, we give others permission to do the same, to let their light shine brightly, and to celebrate their accomplishments, whether it's that they got the garbage out on time or they found the answer to world peace.

### Ask yourself:

- How have I undermined my sense of pride about what I have accomplished and who I am?

- How can I be more comfortable feeling proud of myself and my accomplishments?

- What five things am I the proudest of, and why?

# The Possibilities of Recreating Yourself

For ten days in June, a dear friend and I went on a road trip. Little did we know that the women we met would become examples of the unlimited possibilities that life offers.

One of our stops was Sun Valley, Idaho. Exploring the area, we walked into a lovely art gallery filled with beautiful paintings priced way beyond our budget. The gallery manager explained that twenty years earlier, a young woman, also on a road trip, had stopped in Sun Valley, fallen in love with its beauty, and wanted to stay—but had no way to support herself. So she bought an artist's instruction book, taught herself to paint, and started this gallery.

A few hundred miles later, we were at a ranch in Montana, getting ready to go horseback riding in the mountains. One of the ranch hands shared that she had worked in a high-powered corporate job and had developed serious stress-related health issues. Visiting the ranch on previous vacations, she had fallen in love with the horses, the mountains, and the peace they brought her. Ultimately, she decided to quit her job and work here full-time. Her health issues had now all resolved, and she was feeling better than she had in years.

At our next stop, we met two women at a crowded coffee shop. Seating was limited, so we all decided to sit together. As we visited, one woman shared that she was the first person in her family to graduate high school. She went on to college, then to law school, and became a district court judge. Then her friend told us that she had been a single mother on welfare and was now the chief judge of the juvenile court in her district.

So many inspiring women on one short road trip! They taught us that there is always an opportunity to recreate ourselves and our future.

I thought of them often whenever I doubted that I would ever move forward from the chaos of my divorce.

And even now, whenever I doubt my dreams or doubt myself, the memory of these outstanding women beckons to me, smiling and nodding, and I keep on.

*Ask yourself:*

- Who are the women that inspire me, and how do they inspire me?

- How am I inspiring others?

- If I am able to imagine the possibilities for my future, what do I see?

# Joy and Finding Frogs!

Three little girls, an eight-year-old and six-year-old twins, knelt down by a small pond. They were thrilled that they had spotted a frog and did not want to take their eyes off it.

They yelled to the adults nearby, "Look! Do you see it?" "Come over here! You can see it better!" "Do you think we can catch it?"

The girls knew that frogs were meant to be caught—and never imagined they were meant to be kissed. You don't need to kiss anything or anyone to know you are a princess.

The pond was shallow, and the girls didn't care that they might slip on the edge and fall in. They didn't care if their excited shouts might seem too loud or inappropriate.

As they continued to look into the murky green water, they spotted a second frog, and then a third. The girls were filled with joy at their discoveries, yet their aunt, who had lived near the pond for over twenty years, admitted that she had never seen any frogs.

Though it's a strange analogy and possibly a bit of a stretch, sometimes joy, like these frogs, is right in front of us, and we don't notice it or can't imagine it is there.

Sometimes we hesitate to share our excitement in case we fall or fail in some way, or feel we will be judged for acting inappropriately enthusiastic.

Sometimes we are the ones searching for joy, and sometimes we are the ones offering it to others as we shout, "Look! Do you see it?!"

Either way, once it is seen, the light that joy shines into our lives makes us aware that the more we look, the more joy we will certainly discover.

## Ask yourself:

- Without having to kiss a frog, what makes me know I'm a princess?
- What discoveries have brought me joy?
- How can I make finding joy a habit in my life?

# The Artist in You

One evening I was invited to an event that showcased eight artists, each sharing not only the work they created but why they created it. I was truly inspired and only teared up twice!

Though each person's story was unique, they all explained that their art grew from their life experiences and family histories. They wanted their art to have value and connect people to their own hearts and to each other. They wanted their art to make people wonder and question and explore what it means to be human.

Even though you and I may not paint, dance, sing, or write plays, we are still artists. We are the artists of our own lives, creating unique designs from the elements of our past and from the dreams of our future.

One young woman explained that the way she begins every project is similar to how Indiana Jones crossed a deep chasm towards the end of the movie *Indiana Jones and the Last Crusade.* He is standing on a high, narrow ledge and needs to reach the other side of this divide. But there's no bridge, and crossing seems impossible until he steps out in faith—and when he does, the bridge appears.

As the artists of our own lives, we will often be challenged to step forward in faith, trusting there is a path that will support us and lead us to what we are searching for. Sometimes the path is very clear. Sometimes we only sense it is there. It offers support when we stumble, reassurance when we doubt, and comfort when we feel lost, guiding us always on our unique and beautiful journey in this world.

### Ask yourself:

- When I explore what it means to be human, what do I discover?

- How has it felt when I have stepped out in faith, and what were the results?

- What can I create when I blend my past experiences with my dreams for the future?

# Rush Hour

Monday evening during rush hour, I was running late for an event across town. When I reached the first stoplight, I had a choice. Do I turn left and take the side streets or go straight onto the highway? I didn't see any backups on the highway, so straight it was.

Cruising along for about five minutes, I was thinking about what a smart decision I had made. Of course, you can guess what happened next. The traffic suddenly slowed to a crawl. Ugh!

I was as patient as I could be for the fifteen minutes it took go four miles, and that was it. I took the next exit and got onto a side street where traffic was actually moving. I was feeling pretty smug until a very large, very slow-moving semi-truck turned onto the street right in front of me.

"Really?! Really?!" I shouted. But then I couldn't help myself and started laughing and thought, *Well, the Universe must be trying to tell me something.*

On Friday morning, I had to drive across town again, and this time I would be dealing with the morning rush hour. Before I left home, I had already decided, wisely, I thought, to take the side streets. It seemed like a good idea until I made a wrong turn and then took a detour I didn't need to take. Halfway to my destination, I was waiting at a stoplight and looked up at the highway overpass to see the traffic was flowing just fine.

"Really?! Really?!" This time I wasn't laughing. *What is the Universe trying to tell me?*

Maybe it was simply that no matter how carefully we choose the roads we take in our lives, there will always be obstacles, and life should not be measured by how fast or how efficiently we move through it.

On my way home, I chose an unfamiliar street that turned onto Mississippi River Boulevard. So many trees lined the left side of the road, you might never have known a river was flowing far below. I followed the unseen river to Minnehaha Creek, where I turned onto a quiet side street and followed the creek as it graciously curved through the neighborhood. The entire drive was lovely, calming, and lifted my spirits.

Maybe the choices I make shouldn't be about how quickly I get somewhere—but about how the journey makes me feel. I want more roads like this in my life, and I believe they are waiting for me and for each of us. All we have to do is decide how we want to travel.

## *Ask yourself:*

- How do I usually react when things don't go the way I had planned?

- What major detours have I experienced, and how have they affected my life?

- What gifts have I discovered on detours?

# Shine Your Light

It started with the upstairs hallway light. Sometimes it worked, but in the evenings it never did, and I had to use the light from my cell phone as I went up the steps to make sure I didn't trip on a cat.

Next, the light that hung over my kitchen sink was positioned in such a way that the bulb was exposed and glared right at me. I switched to a bulb with the lowest possible wattage, which eased the glare and, as a bonus, made my kitchen look clean.

Finally, my dining room light fixture simply stopped working.

The brightness in my home had slowly faded, and I had adjusted. Dim light and shadows now became normal.

It never occurred to me that I had spent years living in the shadows of my own life. How often had I dimmed my personal light? Did it start when I trusted the words of others telling me I was not quite good enough? Did I ever believe in myself? I can't remember.

After a handyman fixed the hallway and the kitchen lights and put in a new dining room fixture, I was shocked. The rooms glowed, and I asked him if it was supposed to be this bright and, of course, it was.

Yes, when you decide to let your light shine, it can be startling. It surprises you, and you wonder, "Can I really be that brilliant?"

The answer is, "Yes, you can!" Your family and friends want to see your light. The world needs your light.

It turned out that the old dimmer switch in the dining room no longer worked. I love the thought that once you allow your light to shine, the old issues and old patterns have lost their power, and your light can no longer be dimmed. How great is that!

## *Ask yourself:*

- What is helping me shine my light, and what might be holding me back from shining?

- What is my light helping me see more clearly?

- What is surprising me the most as I begin to shine my light?

# A Most Powerful Resolution

Why do we feel we have wait until New Year's Day in January to make a resolution?

Every day holds the possibilities of a new year. Sometimes new beginnings are bright and feel like sunlight beaming on our faces. Sometimes they are dark, frightening, and even heartbreaking.

Each new beginning offers us the opportunity to choose what is in our highest good. Do we need to exercise or to be still? Can we say no when necessary? Are we able to stop being busy just for the sake of being busy?

Visiting the North Shore area of Minnesota for a three-day vacation, I stopped in the small town of Two Harbors and thought I would never tire of looking at Lake Superior. It was beautiful, powerful, and magical, and I felt it had a sacred spirit. After my short stay, I sensed that if I lived there year-round, dealing with work deadlines, groceries, laundry, bills, and the daily stuff of life, the ever-present lake would become such a familiar part of the scenery, I might find myself taking it for granted.

How much do we take for granted simply because it's familiar?

When we look in the mirror every day, we check our hair, possibly our makeup, and once in a while, we need to make sure there is no spinach in our teeth. But how often do we ever stop to look into our eyes, smile, and blow ourselves a kiss?

You are the most valuable scenery of your life. You are your own Lake Superior, and the most powerful resolution you can make is to not take yourself for granted.

You weather storms. You sparkle in the sunlight. You are filled with beauty, power, and magic.

## Ask yourself:

- What can I do to make sure I don't take myself for granted?

- What does it mean to be the most valuable scenery in my life?

- How do I sparkle?

# THE BABY SHOWER GIFT

One Sunday, I attended a lovely baby shower.

After a delicious brunch, everyone went into the family room to sit and watch the mom-to-be open presents. There were "oohs" and "aahs" each time she unwrapped a gift and held it up for all to see, and I started to worry. What if my gift wasn't good enough, cute enough, clever enough, or expensive enough? What if my gift did not receive one single "ooh" or "aah"?

Were other women feeling the same? Were we all sitting around anxiously wondering how others would judge our gifts?

I convinced myself that I'd made a terrible shopping mistake and wanted to run out and try again.

At state fairs, all sorts of things are judged: cows, artwork, and apple pies. That's how my life has felt, as if everything about me was being judged, and I have simply carried on the tradition of judging myself if no one is available to do it for me.

But life is not about winning, and I decided to declare myself a "judgment-free zone."

At first, I was scared. How would I know if I was acting appropriately or doing what others thought was best if no one was telling me? Then I felt a weight lifting off my shoulders. I would now be the one to decide if I was acting appropriately or doing what I thought was best.

We all have precious gifts to offer, and not just those we bring to a baby shower. We have gifts of creativity, passion, talent, and love, and if they are held up for all to see, we may start worrying about how others will respond, causing us to hesitate sharing them.

Let us each create a "judgment-free zone" around ourselves, so these gifts have room to breathe and expand, to blossom and grow—and so the life we create will make us "ooh" and "aah"!

## *Ask yourself:*

- What things about myself have I judged most harshly?

- How can I become a "judgment-free zone" and how will it help me to not judge others?

- What special gifts do I have that make me "ooh" and "aah"?

# Open the Windows

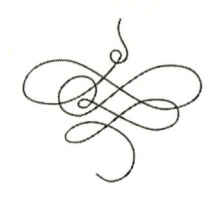

First, there was the long, bitter winter. Then, there was the promise of spring that turned into one more nasty snowstorm. Finally, a summer day came when I could open the windows of my home and let in the fresh air. It was a new season, a new beginning.

Open windows may let in dust and pollen, but they also let in the rich smell of blooming lilacs.

Open windows may let in traffic noise from a nearby highway, but they also let in the music of singing birds.

After a divorce, it can take tremendous effort and courage to "open up." We have weathered so many storms, and often when we thought things were over, there was one more painful blizzard howling through our lives—and sometimes more than one.

In choosing to open up our hearts, we can celebrate the experiences that make us bloom and hear the music of our lives.

Sunday, I was in my home office catching up with work. Laughter was coming through the open window, and I looked out to see that my neighbor across the street was sitting in her yard, potting plants. Two other women were keeping her company and, I'm assuming, sharing potting words of wisdom.

There was another burst of laughter from the group, and I knew exactly what I needed to do. I immediately closed my computer and walked across the street!

The women told me that they saw my window was open, and if I hadn't come outside they were going to shout out, "It's a beautiful day. Come join us!"

When you open up the windows of your home, you will be surprised at the wonderful opportunities that appear. And when you open up your heart, you will hear the chorus of life calling, "It is a new season. There is beauty and joy waiting for you. Come, come join us!"

## Ask yourself:

- What is the music of my life?

- How am I finding the courage to open my heart and bloom again?

- What is calling me back into the world?

# Reflections of the Season...

*Butterflies had to break free of their cocoons...this struggle to break free built their strength and it was this struggle that saved them.*

*We can be compassionate with ourselves when we look back from where we have come and can gaze at the new scenery of our lives and search for meaning.*

*To honor the little girl within each of us, let's choose carefully which voices to listen to.*

*When we choose wisely to depend on things that bring light into our lives, the possibilities for our future are unlimited.*

*We are the artists of our own lives.*

*Can I really be that brilliant? Yes, you can!*

*Every day holds the possibility of a new year. You weather storms. You sparkle in the sunlight. You are filled with beauty, power, and magic.*

*You are the most valuable scenery of your life.*

*In choosing to open our hearts, we can celebrate the experiences that make us bloom and hear the music of our lives.*

# Honoring You

In whatever season of divorce you may find yourself, I honor your courage and strength.

I imagine you standing on the mountain road where another woman once stood. You smell the rich scent of pine trees and the freshness of the open sky. You feel the warmth of the sun on your face and stare at the beauty of the vista stretching out before you. It does not matter whether or not you can see it clearly or notice details.

All that matters is that it is there, your lovely and patient future, waiting to inspire you to move forward into a new life filled with possibilities.